NORWICH CASTLE KEEP:

ROMANESQUE ARCHITECTURE AND SOCIAL CONTEXT

by

T.A. Heslop

Centre of East Anglian Studies 1994

© The Author 1994   ISBN 0 906219 38 8   All rights reserved.

No part of this publication may be reproduced, stored in a retrieval system, or transmitted, in any form or by any means electronic mechanical photocopying, recording, or otherwise, without permission of the publisher. Published by The Centre of East Anglian Studies, University of East Anglia, Norwich. Designed by DT Pro and Printed by The Printing Unit, University of East Anglia, Norwich.

CONTENTS

Introduction   p. 4

Chapter 1:   The Circumstances and
                 Documentation   p. 6

Chapter 2:   The Exterior   p. 15

Chapter 3:   The Interior   p. 38

Chapter 4:   Romanesque Architecture
                 and Social Context   p. 56

Notes   p. 67

Further Reading   p. 69

Glossary   p. 70

ACKNOWLEDGEMENTS

It is remarkable how, in writing even a short book and in a short space of time, one can run up a large number of debts of gratitude. Even paring it to the barest minimum I have to thank Brian Ayres, Nick Arber, Eric Fernie, Olga Grlic, Sue Margeson, Barbara Green, Catherine Wilson, Bill Milligan, Paul Drury, Stephen Ashley, Hassell Smith, Malcolm Thurlby, Larry Hoey, Norma Carroll, Colin Shewring, Chris Edwardes, Michael Brandon-Jones, Dominic Marner, Roberta Gilchrist, Carole Rawcliffe, Richard Wilson and George Zarnecki. The intellectual support of my colleagues in the School of World Art Studies, the financial support of the University of East Anglia with a grant towards my researches into twelfth-century secular architecture and the moral support of my family have been indispensable. Lastly I have to acknowledge the many writers on whose past labours I have been able to found this work.

The engravings from Archaeologia and the watercolour on the back cover are reproduced by kind permission of the Society of Antiquaries.

INTRODUCTION

Norwich Castle keep is the third in a distinguished line of English royal fortified palaces. The two earlier examples, at the Tower of London and Colchester, originated in the 1070s whereas, it will be argued here, Norwich was designed and begun in the 1090s. There were thus some twenty years between them, and this accounts in part for the greater sophistication of Norwich as a piece of architecture. But there is also another reason, apart from simply the passage of time, and that is the very different character of its founder, King William Rufus, so distinct as a patron from his father, William the Conqueror, who had been responsible for the Tower and Colchester.

In this short book we shall be looking at the evidence for the original design and functions of Norwich Castle keep. As will become clear, the aesthetic of Norwich keep is rooted in an environment of increasing complexity in terms of the proportional harmony of the design and its elaborate decoration. Equally, the complex layout of rooms, particularly on the first floor, is probably intelligible only in a context which increasingly preferred the separation of public from private activities and of social space from accommodation for domestic functions such as cooking. A sense of propriety in the segregation of social classes and sexes may also have played its part. That such a consciously elaborate monument was built in Norwich around 1100 is indicative of the city's rapidly increasing economic and strategic importance.

It is, of course, difficult to assess importance objectively across the gap of nine hundred years. What criteria should we use? There are a number of options, one of which is indeed to take major building projects as an indicator. If one does so then it is evident that few cities in England could rival Norwich as a boom town in the late eleventh century, and probably only London exceeded it. The Cathedral and the Castle in Norwich were certainly undertakings on as grand a scale as those anywhere else in the country, requiring many hundreds of boatloads of fine limestone to be imported from Normandy, then to be shaped and laid with a high degree of skill. In addition, the other church building projects of the period in and around the city, while nowhere near so large nor lavish as the Cathedral, indicate when added together a dramatic urban redevelopment which provided Norwich with ecclesiastical amenities on a remarkable scale. The implications for Bishop Herbert Losinga's pastoral care within his cathedral city are manifest elsewhere in the diocese both in towns and in the countryside. When this is joined to the information we have concerning the patronage of secular lords, such as the de Warennes, it becomes clear how wealthy and how significant the region was. We may infer that Norwich was now cast in the role of seat of provincial government to an extent that no single medieval East Anglian centre had hitherto enjoyed.

Much work has been done over the last few years on the development of Norwich, particularly by Barbara Green, Alan Carter and Brian Ayres. Although there is necessarily still much uncertainty, the patterns of occupation and the ways in which several communities scattered along the banks of the river were gradually nucleated to form a single, major centre are very much clearer than they were. The siting of Castle and Cathedral have to be seen in this context, and indeed themselves illumine the whole process of consolidation.

To elucidate the Cathedral's place in the process we now have Eric Fernie's outstanding monograph which exemplifies both the methods by which a single monument can be studied and the light which it can throw on our understanding of the culture and aesthetic of the period. The Cathedral is indeed crucial for our understanding of many aspects of the design of the Castle, and together these buildings raise a question which we shall come to at the end of this study: the extent to which they embody a regional style of architecture. It may seem paradoxical that two buildings so thoroughly "modern" in their international style and their scale should also be fundamentally of their region; but if it is a paradox, then it is one which students of the Romanesque period frequently encounter. For the Romanesque (as we now call it) has the privilege of being the first style name in European art history which has general validity across western Europe. Unlike earlier style names, it does not refer either to a race (such as Celtic), to geography (Insular), or to a dynasty (Carolingian). But though its internationalism is recognised and demonstrable so too is the capacity of Romanesque for being divided by scholars into regional "schools" (e.g. Anglo-Norman, Burgundian, Tuscan). This tendency of modern historians to view the period both in a wide perspective and under a local microscope is, in my view, amply justified by the study of both social institutions and artefacts, as I hope this study of Norwich Castle will demonstrate. It is indeed worth stressing that the Castle itself is as much an institution as an artefact, and in exploring its architecture we will inevitably be considering it as a functioning environment which contributed to and controlled the behaviour of those that lived and worked within it or under its shadow.

CHAPTER 1

The Circumstances and Documentation

The strategic importance and military vulnerability of East Anglia must have been apparent to English government throughout the eleventh century. Before the draining of the Fens, Norfolk and much of north Suffolk was effectively cut off from central England, and access to the region by land could be easily achieved only from the south west, though distances were considerable. Of course access to the region by sea was another matter, but that was a double-edged sword, since throughout the period up to the 1080s the threat of incursion or invasion from Scandinavia was likely to become a reality, and so the region was vulnerable to their seaborne assaults as much as accessible to native support. In 1004 "Sweyn came with his fleet to Norwich and completely sacked the borough and burnt it down. Then Ulfcytel and the chief men of East Anglia decided to make peace with the host, for they had come unexpectedly and he had not had time to gather his levies together".[1] Thetford suffered in the same year and Ipswich in 1010, and it is no surprise that when Sweyn's son Cnut became king of England in 1017 steps were taken to improve regional security. The principal instrument of his policy seems to have been reformed monasticism. Apparently taking monks from the powerful monastery of Peterborough, then under the rule of the energetic abbot Aelfsig, the new king and his queen, Emma, in conjunction with local magnates founded regular houses at St Benet's Holme in Norfolk, in 1019, and Bury St Edmunds in Suffolk, in 1020. It seems from later documentation that the abbot of St Benet's was given charge of the coastal defences of north Norfolk, and his abbey's situation, on the major river system of the Bure, must also have been chosen with control of the waterways in mind (the unthinkable alternative being that it was an open invitation for Scandinavian pirates to sail up to the gates and attack it).

The twenty years following the Norman Conquest of 1066 were just as insecure. Full scale invasion from Denmark was twice narrowly averted, and Norfolk and the Fens were frequent centres of both English and "Norman" rebellion against William the Conqueror. It is in such a context that the Anglo-Saxon Chronicle records in 1075 that the castle at Norwich was held against the crown by Emma, the wife of Earl Ralph le Breton. She soon surrendered it and left the country to join her husband, and this in turn dissuaded the Danish invasion fleet from open conflict with King William's forces. In 1088, following the Conqueror's death, Norwich Castle again sheltered a rebellious baron, Roger Bigod, who was involved in a plot to make Robert, duke of Normandy, king in place of William Rufus.

The castle in question was not the one we see today but its predecessor. The entry for Norwich in Domesday Book adds a little more detail about it: "and on that land over which Harold had jurisdiction there are 15 burgesses and 17 vacant houses which are in the occupation of the castle. And in the borough are 190 empty houses there which were in the jurisdiction of the King and the earl, and 81 in the occupation of the castle."[2] The broad implications of this information are clear; that the castle had been set up within a quite densely built part of the town, possibly within some pre-existing defensive enclosure (if that is what is meant by "in the borough"), and that as a result 98 properties were lying vacant (or perhaps rather that there were no burgesses living in them). But as regards a more detailed interpretation we really are left guessing.

It is generally assumed that the castle in question was on the site occupied by the present structure, and that the mound on which the stone keep now stands is simply an enlargement of a motte built immediately after the Conquest to support a wooden tower surrounded by palisaded enclosures. This is quite probably the correct interpretation, but we need to be conscious of the fact that there is no archaeological evidence to demonstrate conclusively that the present site was occupied by a castle before the very end of the century, or indeed that it fits comfortably with the evidence provided by the documents. Consequently it must remain a possibility that the structures of c.1070 were elsewhere, for example closer to the river to protect the approach to the city up the River Wensum. Whatever the situation was at the end of the Conqueror's reign, it was dramatically transformed under his son, William Rufus, by the construction of a massive stone keep on top of a huge artificial mound.

The decision to provide for Norwich a palatial fortress the like of which could only be seen in England at this date at the Tower of London, apparently finished by about 1097 (by 1100 it seems that Colchester was still built only up to first floor level), has to be viewed as part of a wider strategy. Although even before the Conqueror's death land was being provided to move the see of East Anglia from Thetford to Norwich, it was only with the acquisition in 1094 of the bulk of the vast area now comprising the Cathedral precinct (variously given in the sources as "apud Norwicense castrum" and "apud Norwycum castrum")[3] that the process of endowing the city with the monumental trappings of a major governmental centre began in earnest. A recent study has shown just how often in Anglo-Norman England the foundation of a substantial church was directly accompanied by the building of a new castle (there are some 125 instances cited),[4] and there can be little doubt that the present Castle and the Cathedral were conceived as a "pair" almost from the outset. Quite apart from other considerations, masons' marks on the dressed Caen stone in the lower parts of the presbytery of the Cathedral match those in the keep and imply an overlap in work force and date between the two buildings.

Before the new keep was started however there was

much preparatory work to be done. It has been calculated that about 30,000 man/days would have been required to construct the mound on which the building stands.[5] Even if there was already a motte here, it would have had nothing like the surface area, and probably not the height either, of the present earthwork. That some at least of the mound was new when the keep was built is suggested by the problems caused by differential settlement of the heavy masonry on insufficiently compacted ground. Some difficulties were obviously anticipated by the builders since a giant baulk of timber was embedded in the lower part of the south wall apparently in an attempt to rigidify the structure. However, the fact that a large vertical crack appeared in the north wall near its eastern end suggests that there too the land was only recently built up.

There was, of course, more to the earthworks than just the mound and its surrounding ditch, but there is still discussion about the form and extent of the adjacent bailey(s). The bulk of it was undoubtedly concentrated to the south which was always the principal approach to the site and was where the main gateways and bridges leading to the formal entrance to the keep itself could be found. In a charter of Henry I's reign the church of St John, Timberhill, is called St John "at Castle gate", which gives some idea of the extent of the enclosure.[6] It is tempting to interpret in a symbolic sense the fact that the keep looked towards London. A continuation of the bailey, or a separate and subsidiary enclosure may always have been located to the east of the keep or it may be an early addition.

The audacity of the decision to place the keep on an artificial mound can be gauged in a number of ways. For example at neither the White Tower nor Colchester was any attempt made to raise the building much above the prevailing ground level. The undertaking at Norwich smacks of a devil-may-care hubris which seems to have been typical of King William Rufus. However, though William initiated the project it can not have been very far advanced at his death in 1100, and its completion must have been the responsibility of the royal administration (whether local or central is not clear) of his brother and successor Henry I. Henry visited Norwich at least three times, around 1104, probably in November 1109 with a substantial entourage of notables, and most significantly the Anglo-Saxon Chronicle records that he spent Christmas there in 1121.[7] While it is just possible that the keep was finished for an earlier visit, it seems more likely that the formal inauguration of the great fortified palace would have been timed to coincide with a great Christian festival which was probably also the occasion of one of the king's thrice yearly official "crown-wearings". His second marriage, to Adeliza of Louvain, was less than a year old, and her consecration as queen probably also encouraged the kind of show of fealty for which crownwearings were designed. At a local level too there were changes, for the founding bishop of the see, Herbert Losinga, had died and had recently been replaced by Eborard.

The documentary history of the Castle over the subsequent century and a half reveals a more than usually chequered career.[8] As originally set up, the garrison was in part to be provided by the knight service owed to the king by the great ecclesiastical lords of the region. These were gradually released from obligation, beginning with the monks of St Benet's, already at about the time of the new keep's completion, followed in 1130 by the cathedral (as it was from 1109) of Ely and culminating in King Stephen's charter to Bury.[9] In both of the last two cases the obligation was transferred to the "home" castles of Ely and Bury, and the former case implies that other provisions were being made for manning Norwich. In the case of Bury, the transfer must have had something to do with the civil war which broke out in 1139. For at the beginning of Stephen's reign in 1136, Norwich Castle had been "taken over" by the local earl, Hugh Bigod. He remained one of Stephen's most persistent opponents, and the king may have judged that it was better to keep the 40 Bury knights (who served in quarter year rotation, ten at a time) close by their abbot, who remained loyal, than risk sending them to Norwich.

The situation in Norfolk was very uncertain for two decades, though it improved for Stephen after the marriage in 1149 of his son, William, to the de Warenne heiress, Isabella, who brought her family's major estates and castles in the area even more obviously into the king's camp (her father had been loyal to him). It may have been as a wedding present that Stephen gave his son the castle and town of Norwich. Certainly by the time of his treaty with the young Henry of Anjou in 1153, by which Stephen in effect signed away his son's chances of succeeding to the throne, Stephen could still claim for William "the castle and town of Norwich... and the whole county of Norfolk, except what pertains to churches and prelates and abbots and earls, and excluding particularly the third penny which pertains to Hugh Bigod as earl".[10] The compromise he was attempting between his son and Hugh Bigod was inevitably unsatisfactory since it effectively created two earls for the same county, and they must have loathed each other. It was left for Henry of Anjou to sort out the mess after he became king. Soon after the beginning of his reign, in 1155, he (re)created Hugh Bigod officially earl of Norfolk, but William kept Norwich Castle until 1157 when, in one of those acts of decisive government for which Henry II was to be famous, he confiscated all the castles belonging to both men. He followed this up by ignoring Stephen's charter to Bury and asking for the Bury knights to return to Norwich, which suggests that removing them might always have been regarded as a temporary expedient. Needless to say there was trouble over this too.[11]

The Pipe Rolls, which survive as a continuous

record of governmental accounting from Henry II's reign, reveal various payments for work on the castle. In 1160-61 the burgesses paid 10 marks (£6/13/4d) on unspecified work, and in 1173 £20/4/8d were spent on repairing "the stone bridge, palisade and three brattices" presumably in preparation for the expected invasion from Flanders and the local support it was likely to receive from Hugh Bigod. The account is invaluable because it tells us there was already a stone bridge (presumably across the main ditch onto the mound). Further, the defensive enclosing "walls" were of timber, and indeed were to remain so for another hundred years. However, repairing them was to no avail for the castle fell to the rebels and invaders. Their victory was brief and over the three years from 1174, after the insurrection was quashed, more than £70 were spent on further repairs. Minor expenditure appears intermittently thereafter until 1204-5 when a substantial £85 was expended on repairs and apparently on new work.[12] This possibly included the towers flanking the upper end of the bridge, their circular form would be consistent with such a date, but if the purpose of the alterations was primarily military, as opposed to domestic, it failed to prevent the castle falling to an invading army for a second time in under fifty years when in 1216 Prince Louis of France captured it as part of his attempt to seize control of the kingdom.

It was doubtless one or other of the two sieges that caused the fire damage which is visible in the forebuilding (generally known as Bigod's Tower) underneath the platform in front of the great entrance door to the main hall. The elaborate vault (fig. 9) and a good deal of the surrounding masonry are coloured pink as the result of very intense heat at a height some twenty feet above ground level. Confirmation whether this fire did help reduce the keep or not will depend on archaeological exploration of the north-east corner of the building, but the amount of heat and lack of smoke generated makes clear that the scorching is not caused by a nightwatchman's brasier but by a massive combustion of tinder-dry fuel, and that is quite consistent with siege tactics. It is even possible that some undermining of the adjacent wall into the keep had occurred since there is now substantial later patching in this area.

New stonework in the basement of the keep, for example around the opening towards the west end of the spine wall, might also be indicative of a campaign to repair damage caused by an incursion, either after 1173 or 1216, but equally it could be quite independent of it and be part of a general modernisation of the building. Over all, however, what is surprising about the keep is that there is so little sign of later medieval alteration. This is particularly puzzling in the light of the huge sum of £607/17/- spent in the late 1280s in rebuilding the hall in the Castle (the money is equivalent to annual wages for a workforce of about 200 people). There is not a single, identifiable, material trace of this work in the keep. Since the Norman stonework survives pretty well intact all around the interior we may guess that it was reroofing which was the main cost, but this is just speculation.

More clear cut are developments around the site. After years of repairing the wooden defences, which kept blowing down in gales, a decision was made late in Henry III's reign to provide a stone wall, at a cost of over £500. Immediately upon its completion in 1270 a new "Shire House" was begun for the holding of county courts. Gradually interest seems to have been moving away from the keep, and the record some fifty years later that there was so much decay that the sheriff was obliged to live elsewhere, suggests that the maintenance of the Norman building had been allowed to slide. Repairs around the year 1330 totalling some £72/19/- were the last of any significance recorded. In 1371, Edmund of Thorpe, sheriff of Norfolk and Suffolk, wrote to Edward III, that the castle which the king had committed to him by virtue of his office "is so consumed and spoiled in the houses and habitations as well as in the walls, timber, lead, and also in other things, so that no man can dwell in it for the safeguard of the Castle nor reside for any other occasion".[13] The keep was apparently given up as a palatial dwelling and thereafter became the victim of that combination of neglect, selective demolition and unsympathetic adaptation which has been its unhappy lot ever since.

As a consequence of this treatment it requires an effort of considerable imagination and a degree of expertise to envisage that harmonisation of commodious and well-lit apartments with decorative embellishment which its original patrons, designers, and builders worked so hard to create. It is the purpose of this little book to help in the understanding and appreciation of that monument, which can fairly be called the most ambitious piece of secular architectural design constructed anywhere in western Europe during the early twelfth century.

Despite the documentation outlined in the previous pages, there are many things about the keep that we do not know. There is no record of the name of the architect, but that is no surprise since it is generally true throughout Europe in the Romanesque period that we do not know who designed even the most prestigious buildings. The only hints we have about his origins, training and tastes are to be found in his work, and they suggest a familiarity with contemporary architecture both in England and in western France, particularly around the River Loire and its tributaries to the south of the Duchy of Normandy. There was lively, and often hostile, interaction between the Normans and their southern neighbours at this period, and it is possible to imagine either someone from Maine or Anjou working in the Norman kingdom of England or, just as likely, an

Englishman or a Norman who had first-hand experience of the latest architectural developments in the Loire valley, which was then one of the most important artistic centres in Europe.

The masons who shaped the blocks of Caen stone which were brought by sea from Normandy are equally anonymous. The work was quite highly skilled involving at its simplest using a straight-bladed axe to dress rectangular blocks with smooth surfaces. Cutting mouldings, such as hollows and rolls, or carving capitals required considerably greater expertise. The precision evident in cutting the stones for the doorway to the hall in the Castle keep amounts to virtuosity. It is certain that these masons were working in Norwich itself. Every moulded stone was cut to fit a particular location, and in a building as large and complex as the keep this necessitated their being on the building site. Many of the stones have masons' marks engraved on their surfaces, and from them it is possible to deduce that there was a substantial overlap of personnel between the keep and the Cathedral, with perhaps as many as twenty engaged on one or other project at any given time.[14]

As well as skilled stone cutters, there must have been a substantial force of builders who mixed the mortar and prepared the flint rubble which constituted the core of the walls throughout the building. For even though beautifully faced with cut limestone, inside and out, the bulk of the structure was made from flint. It is very likely that the semi-skilled workforce responsible for this aspect of the enterprise was local.[15] Flint was the principal stone of the region and it would have made sense to employ those who were used to working with it. Also locally based would have been the small army of

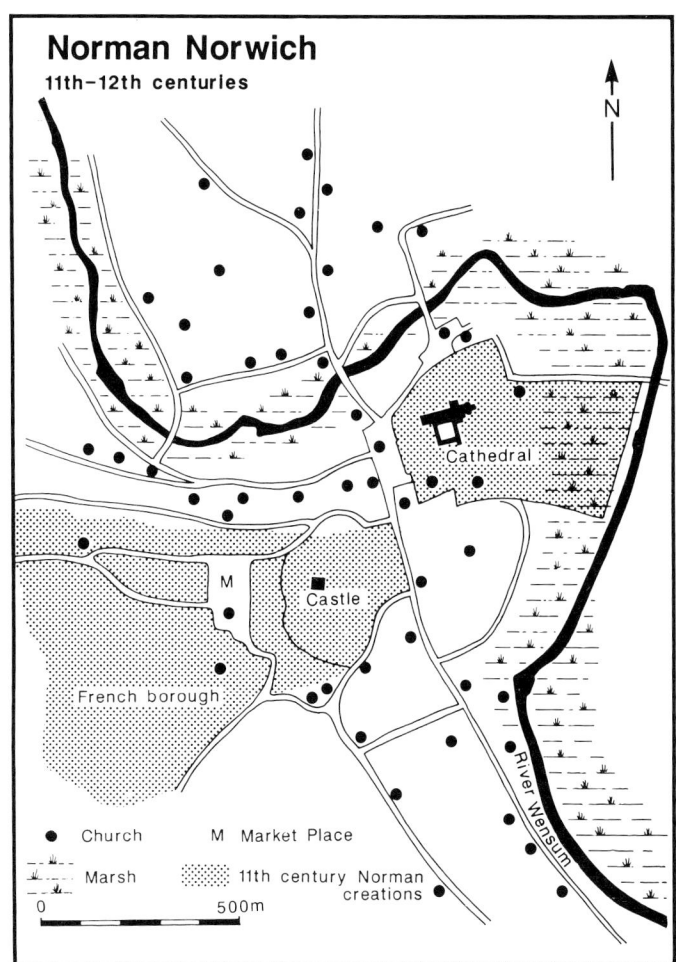

Plan of Norman Norwich. Drawn by Phillip Judge based on research by Brian Ayres.

labourers who must have carried materials and shovelled earth. For even when the great mound and ditches were completed there would have been plenty of back-breaking toil shifting the thousands of tons of sand, lime and stone, and raising water to the top of the great mound. Machinery of any sort was primitive at this date, and the principal source of energy to drive the machines, be they small carts or pulley hoists, would have been manpower.

While it is perhaps not too difficult to imagine the scene as the boats of stone arrived at the quayside, or to imagine the activity up on the mound as the various categories of workers went about their tasks - burning lime, erecting scaffolding, shaping stone - there is a further imaginative leap which is much harder for us to make. For somehow the vision and the intention of the patron, the architect and those co-ordinating the whole project is represented by the building which they constructed. Even if that building had survived relatively unscathed it would require quite careful analysis before we could hope to discern the thinking behind it. As it is, Norwich keep is far from being well preserved, and so before we can begin to place it in its original context we have, effectively, to rebuild it in our mind's eye.

1) The exterior of Norwich Castle keep from the south west.

CHAPTER 2
The Exterior

As we see it today, the outside of Norwich keep is almost entirely a product of the nineteenth century (fig. 1). There are a few original stones on the east facade (where they were originally protected by the forebuilding staircase) and one eroded drain outlet, sculptured in the form of an animal, on the south, but these are almost no help in giving us an impression of the original glory of the exterior. To form any idea of the building as it would have been seen in the twelfth century we have to rely on drawings and engravings made prior to the restorations of the 1830s which so thoroughly disposed of the primary evidence.

In many respects the topographical evidence is excellent. In particular the illustrations made for William Wilkins' paper printed in Archaeologia in 1797 (figs 5-8) and the watercolours, often including measurements, done by Francis Stone in the decade from 1826 (fig. 30) seem to provide about as good a record as one could hope for of a "lost" building.[16] It is however necessary to sound two notes of caution about these sources. The first is that Wilkins himself was involved in producing an imaginative reconstruction since many details had already been lost at the time he wrote. As a consequence some of what he shows is intelligent guesswork, though it is not always clear which bits they are. The second is that rather than making independent drawings, Stone seems to have used Wilkins' engravings as a basis for his own watercolour drawings, sometimes making subsequent alterations, but for the most part simply adding measurements. Nonetheless, with these caveats in mind, we may still count ourselves lucky in the quality of the information which survives.

Before proceeding to analyse the main elevations, a number of general points about the exterior need to be made. To begin with, the variety of the original stonework is not represented in any way by the Victorian refacing. As first built, the keep employed three types of stone, fine limestone from Caen in Normandy, shelly limestone probably from Northamptonshire, and local flint. The core of the building is of flint rubble and mortar, and these materials were also used on the exterior at ground level (up to a height of just over 23 feet) for the main, flat wall areas between the buttresses on all four faces of the building. Quite probably the flint surfaces would have been rendered, but there would still have been a visible difference between the materials of the lower storey and those of the main floor and parapet. As was usually the case in the keep, this difference was a register of function. Because the ground floor was used largely for storage and other mundane purposes, it did not merit the elaboration of the main living spaces.

In general, though, the impression which the exterior gave was of elaborately squared or intricately moulded ashlar blocks. The bulk of these were of Caen stone. This seems to have accounted for all the flat elements of walling from the first string course upwards, and throughout for the buttresses, shafts and arcading. Shelly limestone was probably used, though, for the string courses themselves. This certainly happens inside the building, and is also characteristic of other monuments of the Anglo-Norman period, such as the keep at Colchester. The explanation for this distinction is practical rather than aesthetic, for not only was Northamptonshire stone usually quarried in long slabs suitable for string courses, but it tended to weather better than Caen, an important asset when preparing elements which were to project from the facades.

The net effect of this combination of materials, much as it must have added variety of colour and texture to the elevations, was entirely secondary to the play of light and shade on the exterior occasioned by the blind arcading. From the first string course upwards arcading decorates all the wall surfaces; on north and south facades four superimposed horizontal layers, and on east and west three. The articulating function of these arches will be discussed later but some general points can be made at the outset. The mouldings of the arches themselves and the character of their quasi-columnar supports were subject to a considerable range of variation and permutation. At their simplest the arches have a right-angle section, while a softer and more elaborate version shows a combination of a semicircular roll below a hollow (cavetto) with a quirk between the two. However, the most intricate arches had the roll beneath a right-angled hollow from which emerged a regular series of projections, shaped like faceted tumblers, which reach over onto the roll moulding as though clasping it in place. For ease of reference this widespread motif in the keep will be called "beaker" moulding (fig. 10). In many respects it foreshadows the later English Romanesque use

2) The site of the Castle in the first half of the eighteenth century, before the renewal of the battlements.

of "beakhead" ornament, though it entirely lacks the latter's figurative points of reference. Most of the supports from which these various arches sprang were quasi-columnar, by which I mean that they are cut to look like columns even though they were apparently all, in fact, of coursed masonry integral with the sheer stonework of the facades. A variant of the design was to use a pair of such shafts attached to either side of a narrow pilaster. In addition there was perhaps a non-columnar form of support which may be described as a pilaster with its two edges chamfered at 45 degrees.

Another point which we will do well to bear in mind from the outset concerns the battlements. Their current form is quite out of keeping with twelfth-century practice both because the merlons (upward projections) and crenels (the gaps in between) are quite wrongly spaced, and because the former have arrow-slits in them, and arrow-slits are virtually unknown before the last third of the century. What were probably the original battlements were demolished in the first decade of the eighteenth century because they were in bad repair and threatened to fall on passers by (fig. 2), but in the late 1740s they were rebuilt in the form we see them in Wilkins' and Stone's drawings. Their style as reconstructed in the mid eighteenth century, with more equal spacing of raised merlons and indented crenels (the former without arrow slits), is however a perfectly plausible early twelfth-century design. It also complemented the aesthetic of the rest of the building in that it emphasised the rhythm of the pilasters dividing the bays of the exterior elevations. It is quite probable, then, that the reconstruction was following the pattern of the demolished originals. Sadly, this sensitive restoration was swept away in the 1830s and replaced by the ponderous and anachronistic composition which is still there today. Quite apart from the spacing of the battlements themselves, the insertion of a corbel table beneath the parapet served to increase the visual weight at the top of the design and placed too strong a horizontal division between the battlements and the lower elevation.

It is also worth stressing that the building was without corner towers (a recently published reconstruction drawing mistakenly shows them), and this is significant for a number of reasons. The lack of towers distinguishes the keep from the Tower of London and most other English essays in the genre, linking it instead to a quite different tradition. But quite apart from the sources it implies for the design, it has the aesthetic effect of unifying the facades; there is, as it were, no major punctuation between them either vertically or, as often happens with towers, because the plane of the wall breaks forward to provide support for the extra height. The lack of turrets may well also have had implications for the visual impression that the keep was meant to create.

Having outlined general characteristics of the exterior which apply to all the elevations we may now consider each of them in turn, starting with the south and proceeding clockwise round to the east.

The South Facade

In many respects the south facade of Norwich keep was the principal set-piece of the exterior (fig. 3). As indicated above, the main approaches to the Castle were

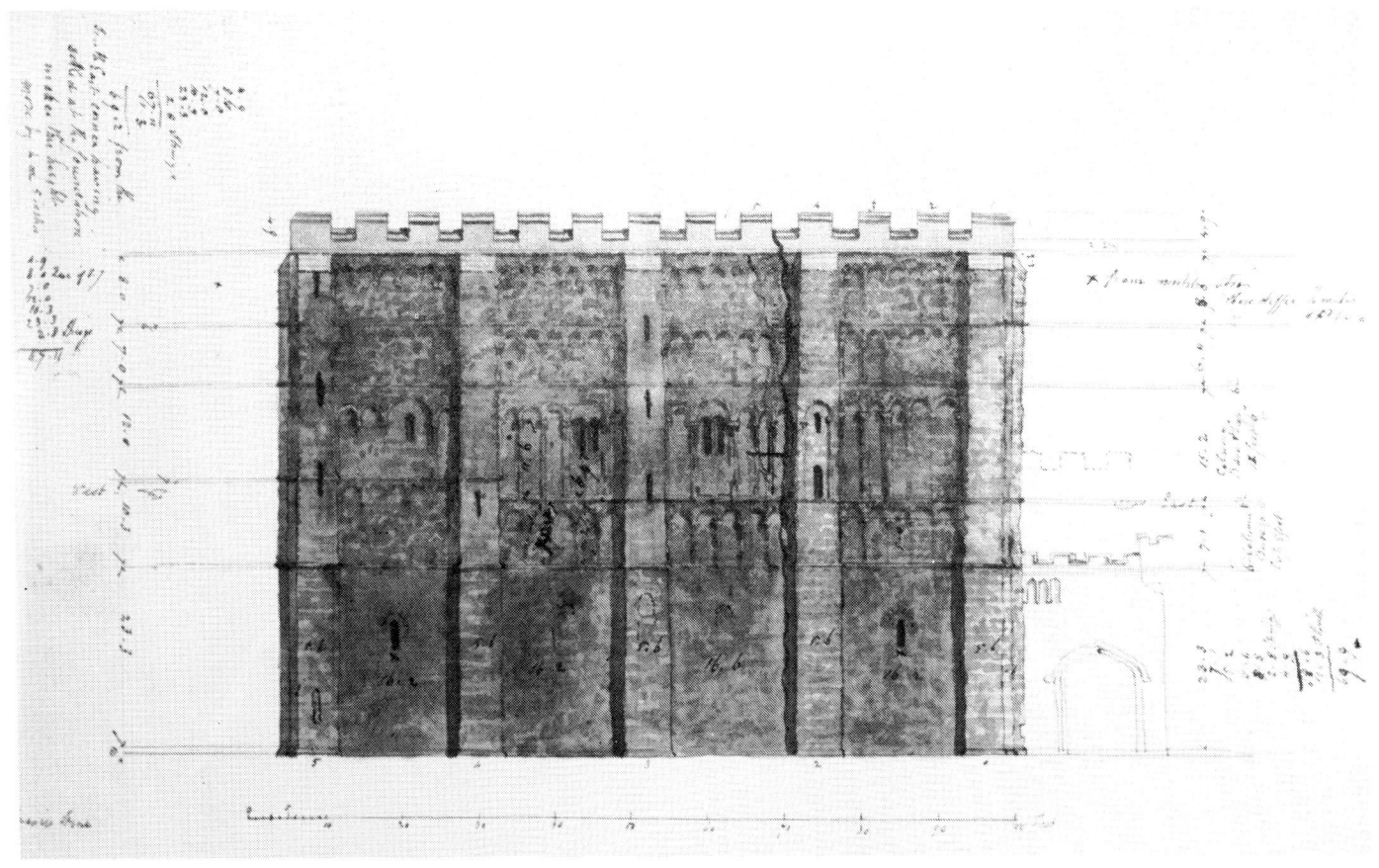

3) Francis Stone's watercolour of the south facade of Norwich keep in the late 1820s. Norwich, Castle Museum, CMN 1922.3.

from that side, and the gatehouse and main entrance to the staircase into the building were part of that aspect. The design exemplifies in its purest form the ways in which a unit of measurement and geometrical proportion were combined in determining the placing of such elements as string courses and buttresses, and it also demonstrates how the different functions and levels of the interior were registered and expressed on the outside.

The sequence of measurements across the facade makes it immediately clear that a simple ratio of 1:3 defined the relationship between the buttresses and the lengths of plain wall between them (fig. 4). Each of the five buttresses (as measured by Francis Stone, and in fact still today) is 5'6" wide, and the spaces between them vary from 16'2" to 16'6", which is three times 5'6". The unit is significant, for 16'6" is an important land

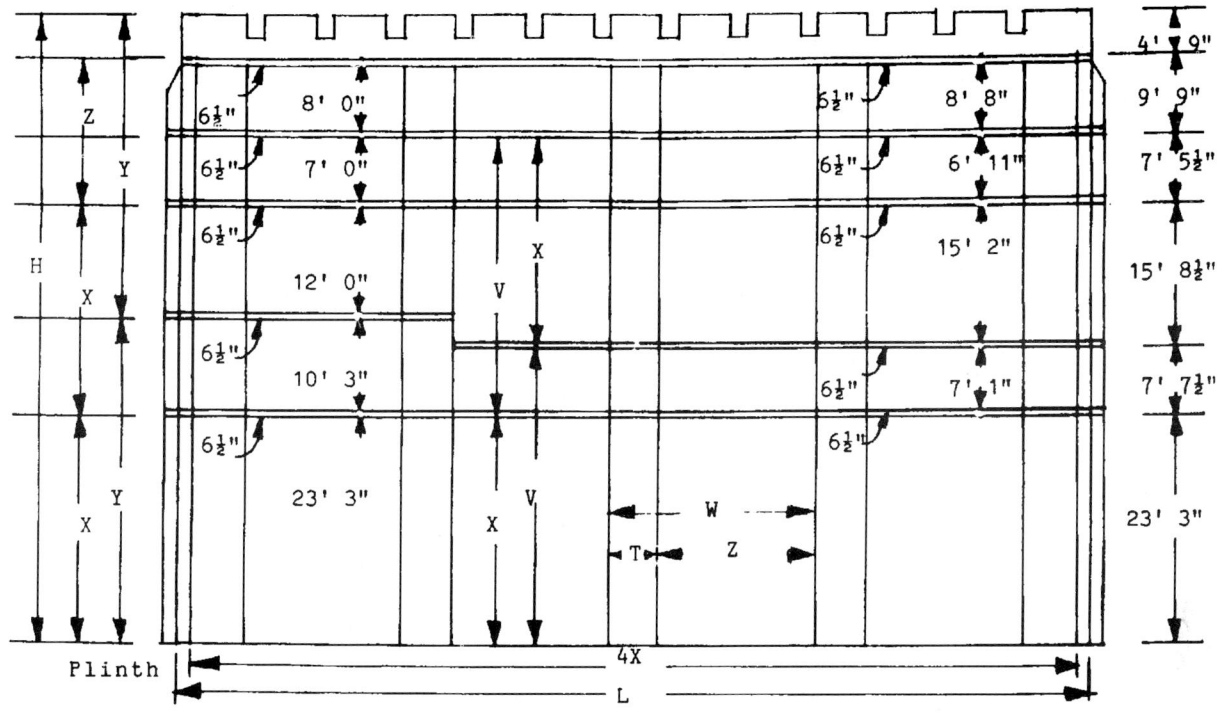

All exterior measurements from Francis Stone (N.C.M. 3.22) 1820s/30s

Z = 3T	L = H√2	T = 5'6"	)
W = 4T	H = 2Y	Z = 16'6"	)
X = Z√2		W = 22'	) NOTIONAL VALUES
V = W√2		X = 23'4"	)
		V = 31'1"	)

4) Measurements taken from Francis Stone's watercolour (fig. 3), and the geometrical scheme on which they are based.

measurement current in England during the middle ages and known as the perch. It is also found in other major buildings contemporary with the keep, most notable Ely Cathedral where it also occurs alongside 5'6", 22' (16'6" + 5'6") and 33" (2 x 16'6").[17] At Norwich keep we will encounter this system of units in the design of the interior as well as the exterior.

But as well as a basic recurrent unit, there was also the ubiquitous appearance of a set of derivative lengths which were used to define the heights of the various string courses of the elevation. According to Stone's measurements, the first string course was 23'3" above

19

plinth level. Since a square with the side 16'6" has a diagonal of 23'4", it looks as though the height of the basement was calculated geometrically from the basic unit. This is confirmed by the fact that the next continuous string course is a further 23'4" above the first one.

These two continuous horizontal lines mark the two major divisions of the elevation and they demarcate the main accommodation space inside the building; the lower one indicating the position of the floor and the upper the springing of the roof timbers. Between these unbroken string courses is another one which changes height for the westernmost bay. In the three eastern bays it is 31' above the plinth. 31'1" is the length of the diagonal of a square with sides of 22', and as each greater unit, comprising a buttress of 5'6" and a 16'6" stretch of plain wall, is notionally 22' across it is clear that this secondary string course height is also derived geometrically from a horizontal length. Furthermore the deliberate choice of this measurement can also be confirmed, as the fourth string course is a further 31'1" above the first one.

The fifth and final string course is placed 16'6" above the third one, so that we have now accounted for all the horizontal divisions on the facade except for one at the west end. Here the second string steps up from 31' to 34'. The reason for the change in this bay on the exterior is that on the interior there is a corresponding mezzanine floor at this level. But the reason that this particular height was chosen seems to have been because it was half the total height of the building in this corner, given by Stone as 67'11". This too is related to the proportional system we have seen in use throughout this facade, for a square with sides of this length has a diagonal of 96', and the length of the whole design is 95'6". Bearing in mind that they had no tape measures, but were reliant on short measuring rods (of 5'6"?) and pieces of (stretchy) rope, this degreee of accuracy is impressive, and demonstrates the care with which the keep was laid out and built. While we do need to remind ourselves at this point that the height Stone was measuring was to the top of the mid-eighteenth-century battlements, there is as we have seen every reason to think that they were a quite accurate reconstruction of the originals. Indeed we can probably add the likelihood of 68' being the correct measurement to the other evidence in favour of the accuracy of the replacement parapet level. It is also worth noting that 68 and 96 are part of a sequence of multiples of 12 and 17 which give a very close approximation in round figures for the relationship between a square and its diagonal (2 x 12 x 12 = 288, 17 x 17 = 289). It would therefore not be surprising if the designer had chosen these numbers of feet for his overall dimensions from the outset.

Once it was established on geometrical principles, the grid (if one may call it that) was given a varied architectural treatment. The moulding of the arcades followed one of three patterns, and the supports on which they rested were possibly also of three types. The lowest order, equivalent to the dado level on the main (i.e. first floor) inside the building, was given quasi-columnar shafting largely composed of coursed ashlar (quasi-columnar meaning with a cross-section which was rather more than half a circle). The arches which rose from these supports were moulded and carried the "beaker" clasps which spanned the gulf between the upper projection and the semicircular roll. This dado order was, then, highly embellished and just as importantly was uniformly detailed across the facade, acting as one of the elements which pulled the design together.

The second order, that containing the window openings for the rooms on the main floor, surprisingly, had very simple arch mouldings, with a plain, rectangular cross section. However, the supports varied, being either quasi-columnar or pilasters with angle rolls on both corners. The latter seem occasionally to have been chosen to give weight and emphasis to outstanding features, such as the windows of the central chamber, but they also appeared, with less obvious justification, on the two western bays of the chapel. There may possibly have been some arcane geometrical justification for this change of rhythm, but as we are wanting detailed, pre-restoration measurements it is unsafe to work on this assumption.

The two upper layers of arcading demarcate the area of wall corresponding to the pitched roof over the southern half of the keep. In other words this wall simply masks the roof and has no tectonic function. Its essentially cosmetic role may explain the extent of its elaboration. There are three distinct zones. The lowest layer is similar to the articulation of the dado level of the main floor in having moulded arches with beaker clasps but, at least as it has been restored, it differs in that it employs chamfered pilaster supports rather than quasi-columns. (However, it must be admitted that the topographical evidence for the original form of this zone offers no clear confirmation of this design.) The middle band, while certainly employing quasi-columnar coursed shafting, has simpler arches, with hollow and roll but without the beaker moulding. The uppermost level is the crenellated parapet discussed in the introduction to this chapter.

In concluding this discussion of the most public facade of the building, it is important to draw attention to the variation in numbers of arches per bay and per storey across the elevation. Here the topographical evidence is in general accord. The basic principle seems to have been that each successive storey had more arches than the one below it. Thus, to take the two central bays, the sequence from main dado to parapet is given as five arches, superseded by five (but including one extra wide arch containing a window), then surmounted by six and seven arches respectively. In the two outer bays the sequence is not quite as emphatic, for although they each begin with five arches per bay, the upper two registers have six each rather than six and seven.

To modern eyes the general effect of this crescendo of busy-ness is to enhance the perspective. However, this potential is largely negated by the pilasters of almost uniform width which frame each bay. It is thus probably more appropriate to the designer's original intention to point out that an increase in the number of openings per bay as the building rises through its storeys is a common phenomenon in Romanesque church towers. It is one of the many hints that the aesthetic of the keep was derived from and intended to rival contemporary ecclesiastical architecture.

The West Facade

The west facade of Norwich keep is the least easy to reconstruct, and for that reason the least easy to interpret. The topographical evidence is often inconsistent and is not always easy to square with the material remains of the building itself. Add to this the inadequacy of Stone's measurements for this elevation and the possibility that this side of the building had perhaps already been restored before he, or even Wilkins (fig. 5), recorded it and one is left with a recipe for confusion. I shall begin with those areas where the evidence is most straightforward.

Like the south facade, the west is divided into four bays by five buttresses. The overall width is now about 89'6" and cannot have been very different before the refacing in the 1830s. This length is broken down into buttresses of 5'6", the unit standard for buttresses on the exterior, and intervening bays, each at present measuring around 14'10" (rather than the 16'6" of the south). At each end is a return of about 1'6". If there is a simple geometrical principal underlying these bay widths, it escapes me.

The vertical measurements do nothing to help elucidate matters. The lowest string course is at 23'3", as on the south facade, though here on the west there is no geometrical justification for it. From that string course upwards we enter a realm of uncertainty as to the actual heights involved so that it would be very unsafe to draw any conclusions about proportions. The next string course was given by Stone as 11'9" above the first. This may be correct, but he also showed it as continuous with the string on the south elevation which he measured at one foot lower. Clearly if both measurements are correct, there must have been a small step up where the string course rounded the corner from one face to the next. However, no such step is shown on any of the drawings or engravings including his own. But there is another, equally serious problem if his measurements are wrong. The total height for the building above the plinth which he gave for the southern corner of the west face, taking into account his 11'9", is only 67'6", whereas a few feet

5) Late eighteenth-century engraving of the west facade of Norwich keep, based on Wilkins' original watercolour. From <u>Archaeologia</u>, volume 12, 1796.

away on the south face it was five inches more at 67'11". Clearly we cannot subtract a further twelve inches from the west elevation without exacerbating an anomaly that may already be due to mismeasurement. Nor is the situation resolved by the height he gives for this element at the west end of the north face, which at 11'3" exactly splits the difference between the two divergent heights he gives for the opposite corner!

The next string appears at two levels; higher in the two central bays, and lower in the two which flank them. In these outer bays we can see precisely what was not visible lower down, a step in the height of the string course at the north and south corners of the facade. No measurement at all is given for its position but, to judge by the scale of the difference on the best representations we have of it, it looks as though it was about 2' lower than the 53'10" given for its height above the plinth in the central bays. If it were indeed at 51'10", we would have here a comparable formula to that being used on the south face. On the west facade, the width of the greater bays (that is a unit comprising a buttress and its adjoining length of flat wall) is 20'4" (5'6" plus 14'10"). The diagonal of a square with sides of this length is 28'8", which added to 23'3" gives 51'11". Thus it looks as though the height of the third string course in the flanking bays does take account of the shorter bay width on the west facade.

In the two central bays of this elevation, however, the upper string course height at 53'10" is comparable with the 54'1" given for the string supporting the highest layer of arcading on the south facade and is therefore not dependent upon or derived from the bay widths of the west face itself. This suggests a desire to re-establish continuity with the south (and as we shall see the north) elevation. The height of the upper arcade in the central bays of the west front, at 8'5", also compares well with the 8'7" given for the same element on the south facade.

The west facade, facing the new marketplace of the city and the "French Borough" founded shortly after the Conquest for the newcomers, is a largely symmetrical design, the two central bays forming a distinctive unit flanked by two rather more irregular bays which are, however, more or less the mirror image of each other. The form of the central bays is partly determined by the latrines built into them at main floor level. Here, the front face of the wall breaks forward to the same plane as the buttresses so as to incorporate the chutes in the wall thickness in such a way that they almost overhang open space. The chutes themselves emerge as four vertical slits beneath the large arch that springs between the buttresses framing each of these two bays. Above the latrines the wall plane is recessed back to its normal position.

The symmetry of this central section is enhanced by the balance of each of its component bays. Each has a large, double window opening in its centre, with five blind arches in the registers below it and, at least according to Wilkins' engravings, five more above it. Unfortunately it is necessary to be rather wary of accepting this scheme as entirely Romanesque. The neatness of the masonry of the central bays shown in some of the topographical drawings suggests that this area had already been refaced by the second decade of the nineteenth century, but it is not yet quite clear when. Wilkins' engraving may pre-date the restoration here, but he himself has indulged in some tidying up. For example, the original disposition of window openings still visible in the interior of the building does not tally with his version of their exterior manifestations, or indeed anybody else's view of the outside. Nonetheless his arrangement can probably be relied upon in its basic form.

The flanking bays also begin at main floor dado level with five blind arches, though the row at the southern end was once pierced for a doorway which must have disturbed the sequence. Above the dado in each bay is again a large window, with double openings divided by a central shaft, but each is off-centre in its bay. Wilkins implies that these were rather lower on the facade than the large windows in the central bays, but this is unlikely to be correct since the openings are at the same height on the original interior wall, which still largely survives. The uppermost layer of arcading has only four arches per bay, also off centre to allow for window openings alongside them, though originally these were not as long as they are shown in the topographical record and may well have been accommodated above the string course.

As on the south facade, the arch mouldings varied. The lower ones had beaker clasps and the two upper registers did not - though more than that is hard to say. There was, however, a most striking use of reticulated masonry behind the upper arcade, a motif which was exactly paralleled on the west front of the Cathedral, but was already promulgated in the transept clerestory there. Altogether, with its central emphasis and symmetry, it is with great church facades that the west face of the keep is most comparable.

The North Facade

The original intention of the designer of the keep was that the north facade should be more or less a mirror image of the south. The principal variations would be caused by the difference in fenestration which was itself a result of the sizes and functions of the rooms behind the facade. As it was actually built, however, there was a far more striking difference, the addition of a sixth buttress in the middle of the second bay from the east (fig. 6). The function of this addition was structural rather than aesthetic, since it served to strengthen the wall at a weak point, where it had begun to split, and also to conceal the damage. Fortunately, as the fissure was near the centre of the bay it was possible to position the buttress equidistantly from its neighbours creating a sequence of 5'6" intervals. Thus a primary unit of measure was respected even though the first design had to be abandoned.

The measurements of the north front, in so far as they are given by Stone or may be deduced from his notes, generally match those on the south and confirm that the geometrical scheme envisaged for these elevations was carried through with considerable accuracy. Stone's drawing of the facade gives only vertical dimensions, and these are incomplete. However, the ground storey is 23'3" as usual, and the upper two tiers (including all three string courses) are 16'5½" at the west end and 16'6½" at the east end of the wall. No height is given for the window zone of the north wall at either end, nor any total heights for the elevation from

6) Late eighteenth-century engraving of the north facade of Norwich keep, based on Wilkins' original watercolour. From <u>Archaeologia</u>, volume 12, 1796.

which they may be deduced. The lower arcading of the main floor is 11'3½" at the west end (as already mentioned), but most unexpectedly is shown as 10'0½" at the east. This latter must be an error for 8'0½". To begin with, the same height is given as 7'11½" on the drawing of the east front, and for another, the proportions of both Stone's and Wilkins' representations indicate that the step down is of the order of 3' rather than slightly over a foot.

Horizontal measurements are wanting on the drawing, but elsewhere in the same volume is a sequence of figures for the north front, beginning at the east end, which confirms that the bay widths were very similar to those of the south facade. The first is given as 22', which must be for a bay including its buttress, and the second is a sequence of three measurements of 5'6" for the aberrant second bay with the intruded buttress;

apparently revealing that the distances between buttresses was the same as the width of the buttresses themselves, which would yield a bay of 16'6". The third bay, and the last one he measured is given as 15'10", which is a full eight inches less than we would expect and, if it is correct, is the first serious "error" we have come across in the laying out of the building.

The overall variation of arch mouldings is like that on the south front. The main floor dado and the lower of the two roof line arcades have the beaker clasps, whereas the other two orders do not. However, the distribution of the arcades was rather more even. According to Wilkins each of the large bays had a run of six arches at three different levels, but though this is true of the two upper layers it is probably incorrect for the lowest level where both Stone and Woodward indicate five arches per bay for the exterior dado of the great hall - and this is indeed the way it was restored in the 1830s. Nowhere is there evidence of the seven arches per bay apparent at the top of the south facade. At main window level in each of the wide bays there were three smaller arches occupying a little over half the width with a larger arch framing the windows. In the two, narrow, 5'6" bays, the system was reduced to a single overarch containing the two smaller arched window openings. In the original scheme, no doubt the great hall would have had three windows, not four as at present, and the single large window in the second bay would have been placed slightly off-centre to the left so that one blind arch appeared to its left and two to its right. There would thus have been two blind arches and a buttress between each pair of large windows, allowing an even spacing on the interior.

The very neatness of this scheme emphasizes the minor illogicality of the south facade where the greater variety in the numbers of arches per bay, across and up the facade suggests either experimentation, a different designer, or different teams of executant masons realizing essentially the same decorative intentions by rather different means.

The East Facade

The design of the east face of the main body of the keep was dominated and substantially obscured by the great staircase and entrance tower which stood against it (fig. 7). They will be considered in the following section, but for the moment we should think them away and analyse the main elevation.

Stone gives the height at the north-east corner as 68'2" above the plinth, which compares well enough with the 67'11½" in the south-west. The components which he quantified have many, by now familiar features. A standard ground floor of 23'3" has a string course and dado arcade of 7'11½" surmounting it. This gives a total of 31'2½", close enough to the diagonal of a square of 22' (i.e. 31'1") which was a determining height for the greater part of the north and south facades. The next

7) Late eighteenth-century engraving of the east facade of Norwich keep, based on Wilkins' original watercolour. From Archaeologia, volume 12, 1796.

string course is a further 17'4½" up the wall which gives a total of 48'7" above the plinth. Since a square with a diagonal of 68'2" has sides of 48'2" it is possible that this is how the height was arrived at (the discrepancy of 5" is still less than 1%). The final layer of arcading on this facade, which like that on the west has only three tiers of decoration, matches the lowest level both in height (8'0½") and in arch moulding (with beaker clasps).

To judge from Wilkins' engravings, the arches themselves sprang from an abacus level defined by the continuation onto this facade of the penultimate string course on the south front. This is an important point to note, for it suggests that main string course heights are not the only horizontal divisions which were taken into account in the planning of the elevations. However, since Stone rarely gives us figures for their positions, we are not able to take their analysis any further.

If the vertical measurements are generally intelligible in terms of the other exterior elevations, the bay divisions are not. The buttresses vary greatly in width and so too do the stretches of flat wall between them. For the southernmost sequence Stone gave 7'3", 12'10", 5'3" and 15'10", a marked contrast from the steady alternation of 14'10" and 5'6" found on the west face. We may infer that this second, very wide bay is to bring the central buttress of the facade into alignment with the spine wall, but it does not explain why the southernmost buttress was so wide, nor the bay adjoining it so narrow, in the first place. Although we may surmise that it was the design of the main entrance stair which was effecting the divisions of the elevation, it is not obvious that this was the case. And paradoxically at the northern end of the facade where the size of the forebuilding (Bigod's Tower) might have been regarded as the determining factor, it does not appear that this has controlled the positioning of the buttresses. All in all it is still uncertain what the imperatives were which led to this facade having such irregular bays.

The topographical evidence suggests that there were also some unexpected variations in the way in which this facade was arcaded. The clearest point, and the easiest to explain, is the pair of blind arches on the wide, southern buttress at first floor window height. This is probably intended to mark out as special the exterior of the apse of the chapel on its eastward facing side, but it also serves to decorate this unusually wide buttress, thus avoiding the display of an expanse of plain surface, which was obviously abhorrent to the builders. It may be for the same reasons that the level above has a single, larger recessed arch, though apparently without supporting colonettes. Elsewhere across the facade the buttresses are left blank except for occasional window openings.

The Entrance Stairway and Bigod's Tower

Two of the most distinctive and innovative features of Norwich keep were the massive stone stairway abutting the east facade and the elaborately decorated

8) Late eighteenth-century engraving of "Bigod's Tower" on the east facade of Norwich keep. From Archaeologia, volume 12, 1796.

forebuilding, known as Bigod's Tower, which stood at its northern end (fig. 8). Large entrance stairs leading to forebuildings were to become commonplace in later English keeps, but around 1100 they were something of a novelty. Norwich is therefore important not only in itself but also as the starting point of an enduring tradition. It is perhaps surprising that earlier castles with great stone residential blocks with first floor entrances, such as the Tower of London or Castle Acre in Norfolk, had wooden stairs leading to a wooden platform fronting the main doorway. One would have expected structures of such pretensions to aim at a uniformly grand image, and perhaps even to lay particular stress on the principal access. But it seems rather as though they were content to take over the wooden stair and platform structure from the first floor hall (which would often also have been of wood), which was itself the building type from which castle keeps ultimately derived.

While there are other ways of interpreting the evidence, it is worth commenting that Norwich keep itself seems, in a number of respects, to acknowledge the character of its wooden antecedents. According to eighteenth-century commentators, it incorporated a drawbridge at the top of the flight of stone stairs immediately outside Bigod's Tower. This seems quite likely; there was certainly a horizontal platform interrupting the stairs at this point, and beneath was an open archway rather than solid masonry. It is hard to imagine what this configuration could imply other than a drawbridge and pit arrangement. Two other features of wooden architecture survive as skeuomorphs. The first is the corbel table below the parapet string course. This decorative device has its origin in the projecting ends of rafters or joists but they are here copied, as elsewhere in Romanesque architecture, in stone. But perhaps the most significant allusion to wood is the way in which both tower and stair are supported. One of the peculiarities of Bigod's Tower is the fact that it is open to the world at ground floor level, almost as though it were supported on posts. The impression is reinforced by the spectacular rib vault supporting the first floor platform (fig. 9), which emphasises the idea that the weight rests on its four corners rather than on any intermediate wall. There were two large openings under the stair itself, though perhaps only one of them was open to the east. Here too, it is as though the skeletal structure of a timber framework underlay the conception of the whole entrance.

Such an approach was a solecism in later castle architecture. It contradicted the image of solidity and impregnability which was so much a part of a castle's image and, worse still, it provided a convenient shelter for an aggressor where he was out of sight of the defenders and could, with impunity, undermine or excavate the wall of the keep. In the case of Norwich, the wall was even more vulnerable because it was much reduced in thickness by a mural passageway from the base of the spiral staircase in the north-east corner. It is not surprising that the wall was indeed broken through at this point (though quite when and under what circumstances remains unclear) and it is significant that

9) Rib vault supporting the main floor in "Bigod's Tower".

there are widespread traces of fire damage on the upper walls and undersides of the rib vault.

There are then grounds for seeing the great stair and forebuilding complex at Norwich as a design based on wooden antecedents since as yet there was no established tradition in England for building access to first floor entrances in stone. By the latter part of Henry I's reign a less vulnerable design had been constructed at Rochester which was to set the pattern for subsequent essays in the genre. But if Rochester lacked the defensive shortcomings of Norwich, it also lacked the decorative potential. The great archway under Bigod's Tower had at its springing point at either end a large low relief carving of a lion (fig. 10). Their scale can be judged only by reference to the rather imprecise eighteenth-century engravings of the facade as a whole, but they were at least three feet wide and two feet high, and possibly half as big again. They can be regarded as guarding the entrance and may possibly even be used in a quasi-heraldic fashion, though this is a quarter of a century before the first clear evidence that lions were associated with the royal arms. But the greatest display on the exterior of the entrance complex was not achieved by allusive sculpture but by the elaborately moulded openings of the first floor of Bigod's Tower.

As on the other major elevations so too on the forebuilding, a relatively plain ground storey gave way to arcading above. At dado level on the first floor there was a sequence of paired blind arches, separated from each other by a very short stretch of plain wall (tantamount to a pilaster) but linked by a long abacus spanning the gaps

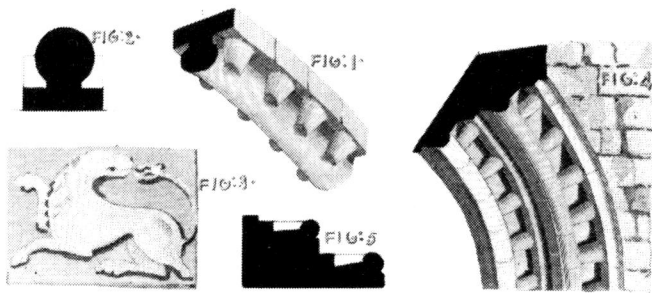

10) Beaker mouldings and lion relief, details from "Bigod's Tower". From <u>Archaeologia</u>, volume 12, 1796

31

between adjacent units. The arches themselves were moulded, probably with a hollow and semicircular roll. The three main openings above the dado on the east front were of three orders. Particular emphasis was placed on the central opening, which was framed by three columnar supports as against the pilasters on the outer order at either end. The arches above were all moulded, the two outer orders with beaker clasps, and the composition was further embellished by the corbel table mentioned above. The richness of this composition foreshadows the great Romanesque gate into the monastic precinct at Bury St Edmunds which, some quarter of a century later, represents the maturity of the Anglo-Norman style in the East Anglian region.

The architecture of Bigod's Tower is in many ways typical of gateways and entrances. One may indeed wonder whether the elaboration of the rib vault to its ground storey would not have been more appropriate to a space which people walked through rather than, as it was, a giant dead end. The envisaged function of that space is a conundrum as, only slightly less so, is that of the main floor above it. Of course, in one sense it serves as an entrance vestibule, but it is not obvious why it has such large openings. There appears to be an inherent contradiction in providing a drawbridge for security on the staircase while having such enormous apertures in the area beyond it. Furthermore, the rigours of the Norfolk climate - particularly the not infrequent east winds - mean that the east facing open loggia is also poorly suited to provide protection against the weather! A loggia of something like the same kind may be found fronting the early ninth-century Visigothic royal hall near Oviedo in northern Spain, a more obviously appropriate climatic context, and one without Norwich's military associations.[18] And if one wishes to find a precursor for the great arch beneath, perhaps the closest parallel is at the mid-eleventh-century imperial palace at Goslar.[19] Ultimately the only perspective from which it is possible to make much sense of the forebuilding at Norwich is as a piece of architectural image making almost unrivalled among the castles of Romanesque Europe. But then given what has been said already about Norwich keep, that should perhaps come as no great surprise.

The forebuilding and the stair had already been swept away and replaced by the time Stone came to measure the fabric in the 1820s and 30s, and so he made no record of them. Fortunately Wilkins had published dimensions for the former on one of his engravings (fig. 8), and these indicate that Bigod's Tower was 27' from north to south, 14' deep, and just under 48' high. With the possible exception of the last of these lengths (which relates to the overall height of the keep as the side of a square to its diagonal) none of these derives from the unit lengths or the geometry of the adjacent building, and as a consequence none of the string course levels ties in with those on the keep proper. This tends to confirm the general impression gained from the topographical record that the forebuilding was always intended to be seen as a rather separate, set-piece design linked to the main building primarily by the repetition of architectural motifs and moulding profiles. But the complexity of the loggia openings, the sculpted lions, and the fact that its ground floor walls were of dressed stone rather than rendered flint all serve to set the entrance apart and to draw particular attention to it. As forebuildings became widespread in later decades, the desire to draw attention to them faded just as the desire to make the more secure increased. We are fortunate in having evidence from Norwich of a crucial moment in this process of development.

The Doorway to the Keep

The transition from the outside world to the interior of the keep was marked by a doorway at the top of the main stair inside the forebuilding (fig. 11). It remains one of the least damaged and most impressive parts of the original building - heavily moulded, with three orders of arches and with sculptural embellishment of remarkable refinement for its period. Indeed in its ambition, it has no rivals in England in the first decade of the twelfth century either in secular or religious architecture. Not until the carving of the cloister doorways at Ely, probably about ten years later, is there surviving evidence of so much thought and attention being lavished on a portal.

Beneath a great, blind overarch 16'6" across is the entrance itself and, alongside it, a narrower blind arch which is also given quite elaborate treatment. This pairing of larger and smaller arches is reminiscent of city gates - one arch for the main road and the other for pedestrians. The arrangement was widespread in Antiquity, and it may well be that a deliberate echo of the ancient world is intended here. It is evident that the smaller arch serves no other purpose than to call to mind such compositions.

The geometry of the whole ensemble is a tour de force. Suffice it to say that the dividing line between the larger and smaller arches is at the point which cuts the diameter of the overarch in the proportion one:root two minus one, that the width of the smaller arch is the same as the width of the door opening and that the opening is twice as high as it is wide.

The mouldings are also handled with that combination of sophistication and singlemindedness which distinguish the design of the keep as a whole. Each of the three orders of arches around the door has a roll moulding on its face, but they diminish in diameter from outer to inner arch. The outermost order is otherwise quite simply decorated with projecting studs or bosses. The middle arch has a hollow profile on which are similar bosses, but between each pair of them is an almond shaped cavity fringed with leaves which creates a

11) Mid-nineteenth-century lithograph of the main doorway to Norwich keep.
From Samuel Woodward, The History and Antiquities of Norwich Castle, 1847.

sequence of shadowy interludes across the surface. The innermost arch takes the creation of tonal contrast even further. The alternation of beaker projections and intervening depressions is of a density which produces an almost staccato succession of dark and light, though the sharpness of the contrast is softenend by the faceting of the beakers. Two related changes are thus taking place between outer and inner order of arches. One is an increase in detail and refinement the other in chiaroscuro. Both can be seen as preparing the visitor visually and psychologically for entering the keep. The light levels of the interior, though high by the standards of their day, would have been quite dark by comparison with the outside world, and also would have shared some of the dappled qualities of the inner arch order. Perhaps too the sophistication of life within the keep was being hinted at by the greater complexity of the inner arch moulding as opposed to the outer arch, which was plainer and physically closer to the outside world. Such an interpretation is not meant to imply that the conveying of this message was consciously planned by the designer. But it is clear enough that the sequence of arches was contrived like this because it was felt to be appropriate, even if he was not quite sure why it was appropriate.

The figural elements of the doorway reinforce the idea that the character of the keep and lifestyle of those who inhabited it was very much in the minds of the builders. Of the four voussoirs containing motifs other than foliage or interlace, two have parallels in the borders of the Bayeux Tapestry.[20] One shows the peculiar image of a man on his knees, holding a shield and sword (fig. 12). He has no adversary on the Norwich doorway whereas on the Tapestry he confronts a chained bear. It may be that it represents a some episode in legend, or a contemporary "sport", or that it is proverbial. Whatever its original context, though, it seems from the circumstances of its use to have been current in the secular rather than the religious imagery of the period, and this is supported by the version of the subject on a capital from King William Rufus's Westminster Hall.[21]

12) Voussoir from the inner order of the main doorway to Norwich keep: the fighting man on his knees.

The winged horse near the apex of the arch is presumably the Pegasus of Greek myth (fig 13). This was the warrior-hero's steed which aided Perseus and Bellerophon in their victories over monsters. In the Bayeux Tapestry a pair of winged horses appears on one occasion only, and that is over the head of Duke William

13) Voussoir from the inner order of the main doorway to Norwich keep: Pegasus.

as he and his troops ride into battle at Hastings.

Fighting was the fundamental attribute of the knight's calling, but other pursuits marked out both the prowess and privilege of the warrior elite. Hunting was principal amongst them and the capitals to the left of the doorway show stag hunting and boar hunting, both of which were dangerous and aristocratic pastimes (fig.14).

14) Capitals from the left side of the main doorway to Norwich keep showing hunting scenes.

It is possible that the latter scene is again mythological, representing the hero Meleager killing the boar of Aetolia. Certainly the poses of both the boar and the spearman can be closely paralleled on classical Meleager sarcophagi. Sadly the capitals to the right of the doorway are badly damaged, though there is little sign that they were as pertinent to the self-image and aspirations of the keep's inhabitants. Nonetheless, the overall impression given by the figurative sculpture on the doorway is that the carvers were well aware of the kinds of visual references which would appeal to the users of the building.[22]

It is difficult to judge the relative importance of simple subject matter - man with sword and shield, men hunting - against the possible allusion to mythology. But the presence of Pegasus should allert us to the possibility that various other elements were there to be seen as references to the valour of heroes ancient as well as modern. And once we allow that the details of the sculpture may point in this direction, we can consider again at the overall composition of the doorway and the possibility that it deliberately recalls Roman city gates. For if parts of the architecture are indeed intended to speak a classicising language, then it increases the likelihood that the whole structure might have been viewed in these terms. The proliferation of columns on the exterior is certainly more reminiscent of Roman monuments such as the Colosseum than of anything produced in Europe in the next thousand years up to the High Romanesque period.

Although there is no surviving monument from Antiquity which provides a convincing visual model for Norwich keep as a whole, many of the characteristics of the design can been seen as interpretations of ancient theory and practice. For example, the treatise on architecture written by Vitruvius, and dedicated to the

Emperor Augustus, contains very much the same stress on symmetry, on units of measurement and proportion which are found embodied in Norwich keep.[23] And one way of interpreting the variation between the three different sets of arch mouldings used on the exterior is as a response to the classical orders, Doric, Ionic and Corinthian, described by Vitruvius and visible in impressive remains such as those of the Colosseum in Rome.[24] Copies of Vitruvius were available in Norman England and, though it remains no more than a tantalising possibility that his treatise was influential on architectural practice at the time, one can argue that if it did have an effect it is likely to have been felt in the most elevated and pretensious quarters of the construction industry, in the office of those who designed and built for that latter-day Augustus, the king himself.

CHAPTER 3
The Interior

For the modern day visitor to Norwich Castle, the task of envisaging the original arrangement of rooms inside the keep is very difficult indeed. All the main internal dividing walls have been removed at one time or another. The lower wooden floor, inserted in the late nineteenth century, is at a height which bears no relation to any feature of the medieval building. And the upper wooden gallery, although at the same height as the main twelfth-century floor level, only runs around the outer edge of the building instead of spanning it from end to end and side to side (fig. 15). In other words we are left with a shell which has been refurbished in a way which makes almost no concessions to the form of the original. Indeed it is

15) The interior of Norwich keep from modern floor level looking north west, showing the Victorian roof, gallery and central arches.

almost perverse in its misrepresentation of it, so that, for example, in place of the solid spine wall which originally divided the interior physically and visually, there is a great open arcade which misleadingly opens up the interior and, as we shall see, completely destroys the proportional harmony intended by the Romanesque designer.

Recreating in the mind's eye the ten or so discrete

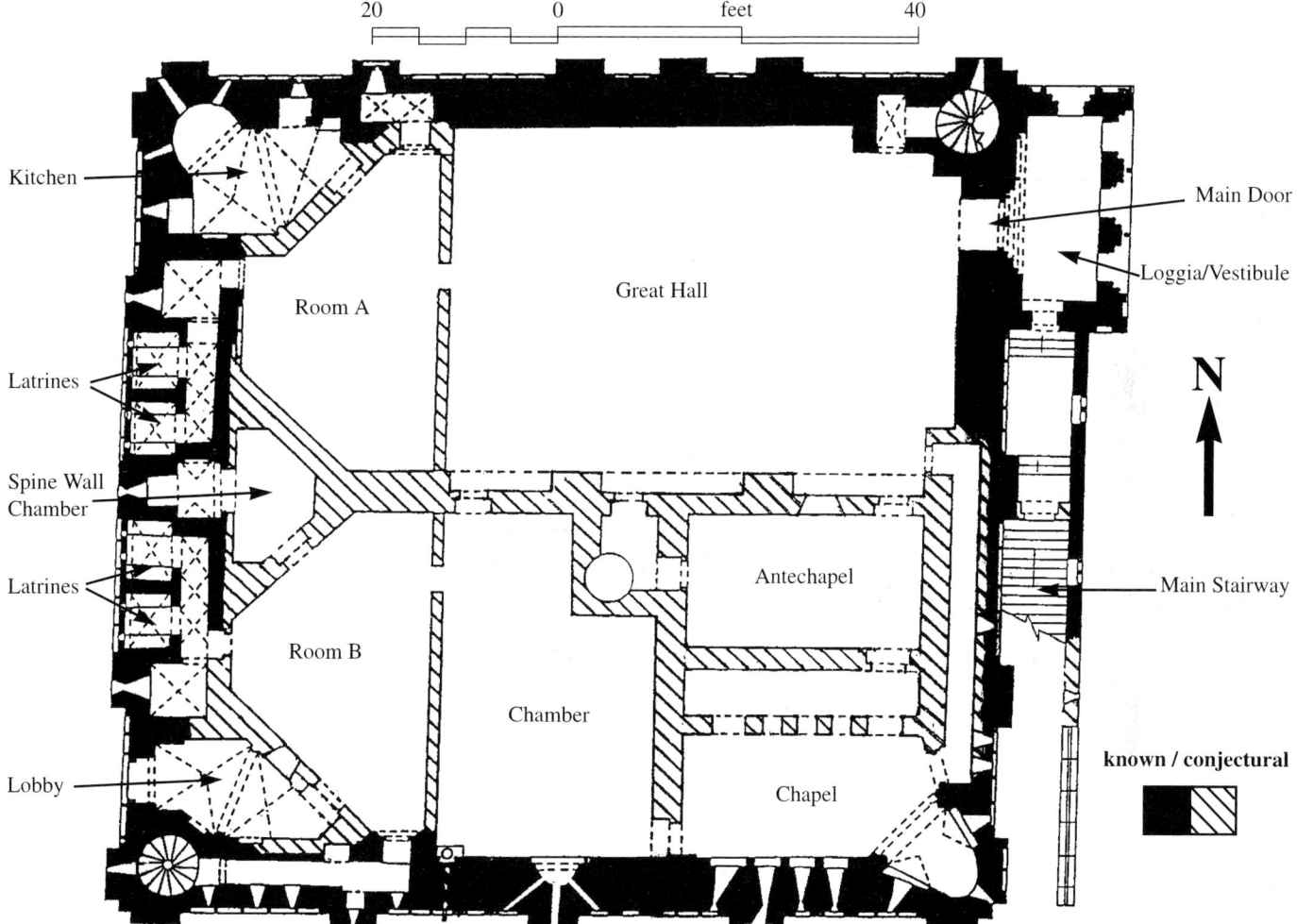

16) Plan of the main floor of Norwich keep

room spaces of the main floor and its mezzanines requires a considerable effort of concentration. However, with the aid of the plans and drawings in this book, the brief descriptions, and a careful examination of the surviving fabric, it is possible to get some idea of the former layout. With that mental reconstruction will come an awareness of the social and domestic functions of the rooms, their relative importance in terms of size and decoration, and some sense of that mixture of elegance and majesty which the greatest creations of Romanesque architecture can convey.

The account that follows will, as far as possible, proceed from room to room, describing how the original layout would have looked and indicating the surviving evidence for the reconstruction of the interior. The description should be read as the verbal accompaniment to the plan of the proposed reconstruction (fig. 16). Much that happened on the main floor was already anticipated in the layout and design of the basement, but that will be dealt with at the end since much of it can only be understood in the light of the principal domestic arrangements above.

The Great Hall

The elaborately sculpted portal in the forebuilding leads straight into the great hall (fig. 17). The floor area of this space was over two thousand square feet, that is to say, the room was 55' by at least 37', though there are reasons for thinking that in places it was nearer to 39' wide. Along the north wall (i.e. to the right) there is still surviving a dado string course surmounted by a wall passage containing four large windows. The windows in the north wall were one of the principal glories of the hall, singled out for decorative embellishment in the form of beaker mouldings on a soffit roll of the framing arch which visually surrounds them. There were two probable reasons for drawing particular attention to these

17) Visual reconstruction of the interior of the great hall of Norwich keep as it might have looked c. 1120.

openings. In a secular context at this period (c. 1100) they were very large, considerably bigger than the windows of any other hall we know about before the late twelfth century. And they most probably faced and gave light onto the high table, set up along the south wall of the hall. The central pair of windows is rather smaller than those at either end, but this is because a change of plan due to subsidence in the building meant that an extra buttress had to be added on the outside, effectively limiting the width available for the window openings in the middle of the elevation. It is likely that when first conceived, there were to be only three windows, all with the same dimensions.

To the west, facing the person entering the hall, was a partition wall some 17' high, probably of wooden construction and running the whole width to the space. It effectively masked rooms further to the west on two levels, the upper being an arrangement of triangular mezzanines. At main floor level near the centre of the partition was the doorway leading to a semi-octagonal room which itself led into the kitchen and the latrines. Visible above the parapet of the partition, a symmetrical composition of five windows dominated the west wall. Of the lower pair only their upper halves would have been seen from the hall, but the central opening would have been entirely visible, and so too probably would the upper pair, discernable below the densely grouped tie beams which probably spanned the roof trusses at about half their height (that is, if the structures of the roofs of Norwich, Peterborough and Ely cathedrals are anything to go by).

The southern boundary of the hall was the spine wall, now disappeared without trace. Although in the circumstances any comments on it are sheer speculation, there are two reasons for thinking that it might have contained a substantial niche or even a row of niches recessed into it. The first is the proportion of the floor space. A square which has a diagonal of 55' (which is the known length of the hall) has a side of just under 39'. This is half of the 78' width of the whole interior at this point, but the thickness of the spine wall would have reduced the available spaces to the north and south to about 37'. One way of overcoming this problem (it was a problem if the designer felt that the principal space should use the same proportional system which determined so many other major features of the building) was to hollow out the spine wall with recesses which would effectively reclaim the missing 2' width. A second advantage would have been to provide decorative incident facing the row of windows in the north wall and an architectural backdrop for the site of the high table. In support of such a reconstruction, it may be urged that the great hall in the keep at Castle Rising in west Norfolk, a design which derives in most respects directly from Norwich, originally had a pair of large niches placed in the spine wall in just this way.

The fourth side of the rectangle, the east wall, still survives almost intact. At its northern end, just inside the main portal, is the entrance to the staircase in the north-east corner of the building which gives access up and down the whole height of the keep. The wall passages which issue from the stair along the north and east walls contain the windows (already discussed on the north wall) on one side and arched openings looking down into the hall on the other. On the east wall these are much plainer than on the north, having simple rectangular sections as opposed to the soffit roll and beaker mouldings of the north wall. This relative informality is further indicated by the changes of level and lack of symmetry in the arrangement of openings here. To some extent this was beyond the control of the designer. For example, the fact that Bigod's Tower abutted on the outside meant that it was not possible to put windows at mid-height in the northern part of the east wall. One is inserted at a rather higher level, and another potential site was left blind because of the obstructions on the exterior. The exigencies of the exterior determine much of the interior of this wall. The uppermost opening is centred on the buttress, but as that is not centred on the hall, the window appears off centre inside the building. Where the east wall eventually clears the obstacles of buttress and Tower, it encounters the rhythm of the blind arcading which again prevents a regular placement of windows to light the hall inside. Most if not all of these problems could have been overcome had the designer chosen to give the east wall interior priority over the exterior. But this was not the case. The east wall attracted least attention within the hall - it was behind you as you entered and there was no focus of interest to it. Even the inside of the main portal is left plain. Once having entered the hall you were encouraged to stay in it, or to move on to other rooms in the keep. There is nothing done visually to encourage you to turn round and retrace your steps towards the entrance.

Apart from the stair door and the main portal there were four or five other doors leading from the great hall. One, already mentioned, must have led into the service areas to the west, but there were probably also entrances directly into the chamber, the well room, the chapel antechamber, and possibly indirectly into the chapel via a passage in the thickness of the wall. All of these were in, or immediately adjacent to the lost spine wall so that it is impossible to reconstruct them. However, with the exception of the entrance into the well room, it may be that their disposition is reasonably accurately imitated at Castle Rising.[25]

The Great Chamber

The central section of the southern compartment of the keep was given over to a large room some 37' by 23'6". As one entered it from the hall, the principal architectural impression of the interior was dominated by the symmetrical composition of the south wall, with its large mural fireplace in the centre flanked to either side by a substantial window at wall passage level (fig. 18). Beside the windows were the points of junction where the lateral screen walls met and framed the south wall. The lateral walls were screens in the sense that although they rose to a height of some 17' on the west and 19' on

18) South wall of the chamber in Norwich keep.

the east, this was still well short of the roof structure. No doubt the decision to leave the chamber open on the sides was taken to allow borrowed light from the windows in the east and west walls of the keep to permeate into the space. The eastern partition was not, however, high enough to prevent the chamber being directly overlooked by people standing on the mezzanine above the chapel, but then privacy in the chamber cannot have been a major issue since the wall passage which encircles the entire building runs along the south wall of the chamber and would have given a good view down into the room to anyone who was standing in the window openings at that level.

Although the composition of the south wall is symmetrical, the effect of its balance is marred by the fact that it is not in the middle of the available space. Masonry scars at window level suggest that whereas the western window stood some 2'6" from the western corner, the eastern window was hard up against its neighbouring wall. The effect in the south-eastern corner would have looked very cramped, and I suggest that in the original design it was also intended to have a 2'6" margin. There is mathematical and structural, as well as aesthetic support for this proposal. The principal fixed point in the composition is the fireplace because it uses the central exterior buttress as its chinmney. The distance from the centre of the fireplace to the western partition wall is 13', and since these positions seem to be those originally envisaged we may surmise that the south wall was to be 26' long. As it was also 26' from the south wall to the projection surrounding the well shaft, the free floor space in the room would have been a square. The distance from the south wall to the spine wall, which formed the northern limit of the room was about 37', and as 36'9" is the length of the diagonal of a square which has a side of 26' a chamber with these dimensions would be entirely consistent with the designer's predilection for this proportion in other important parts of the building. The structural evidence for a major change of plan in the alignment and size of the chapel is largely to be found at basement level, and we will consider it in due course, suffice it to say that it was apparently a decision to enlarge the chapel by extending it westwards which spoiled the symmetry of the south wall of the chamber by slicing about 2'6" off its eastern side.

Despite this departure from the original scheme, it seems that the alteration was managed to be consistent with measurements prevalent elsewhere in the building. The width reduction of the south wall of the chamber probably turned it into a square of about 23'4". Although the overall height is difficult to confirm because of uncertainty about the precise placing of the rafters, there is some supporting evidence. The fact that the string course on the wall starts at 9'8", and that this is the length that results from dividing 23'4" in the proportion one:root two, would tend to confirm that the main storey was the same notional height inside the building as it was on the outside. The string course on the north wall of the great hall was probably also 9'8" above original floor level which also lends credence to this suggestion. Thus it seems that even when diverging from the carefully calculated harmony of the first design, heed was paid to the mathematical principles that had guided the project from the outset.

To the right of the fireplace in the south west corner of the chamber are the remains of a sink built into the wall at waist height. On the exterior of the building the drain, supported by a worn, though still impressively large lion corbel is one of the few surviving original features. It is not obvious why the chamber was thought to be the most appropriate place for a water basin, but presumably it was used for the washing of hands, rather than in the preparation of food.

The existence of the sink must be seen in conjunction with the well, situated in the opposite corner of the room, where it was probably enclosed within a "room" of its own. It is one of the most striking features of Norwich keep that, so far as we can tell, the water services are concentrated in the chamber. This must have been inconvenient for some purposes, for example cooking, but we need to remember that the decision to incorporate a kitchen in the building (in the north-east corner) was taken long after work was begun, and presumably the well was already largely constructed by then. The other imponderable is the use that might have been made of cisterns in other parts of the keep to store rainwater collected from the main roofs. The well is very deep, and it must always have been a chore to raise quantities of water from it. It may be that it was envisaged primarily as a backup system should the rainwater tanks fail, or that it was reserved for food and drink, not for washing. Until more is known in general about the provision of water supplies at this period it is not possible to do more than speculate about the possible arrangements at Norwich.

The Chapel

In the south-east corner of the chamber was a doorway

into the chapel. One jamb of the opening is still visible in the south wall of the keep. The south wall bears many other indications of the form of the chapel: the pilaster arcading of four bays each originally containing a window and, in the eastern corner, the apsidal, vaulted altar space, with its elaborate entrance arch with sculpted capitals. Most significant for understanding the initial impact of the chapel are, however, the traces of joist holes along the south wall above the arcade. These indicate that the nave of the chapel had a flat wooden ceiling about 15'6" above floor level. It is the first space we have yet entered which was not open to the main roof, and this must have effected the light levels as well as the overall sense of containment experienced by the visitor. It must also have helped to focus attention towards the altar space.

For all its apparent logic and sensitivity, the organisation of the chapel does raise some questions. Perhaps the most pressing is why the altar space is at 45° to the nave rather than, as one would expect, a direct continuation from it. The answer appears to be that as first designed, the nave of the chapel would have had a triangular floor plan, and the sanctuary would have been at its apex. The evidence for this extraordinary arrangement is largely to be found in the basement and will be considered later in this chapter. For the present we shall consider the form in which the chapel was built.

The position of the north wall of the chapel is not known, but it presumably rested upon the massive wall at basement level in the keep. That wall is 10' thick, far thicker than it need be for any weight supporting function it can have had. However, if we envisage a north aisle in the chapel then its width serves an obvious purpose: to support an open arcade above its south face and the main north wall of the chapel above its north face. This would allow for a north aisle of about 6' in width, and it would turn the floor of the nave (with its aisle) into something like a square, about 27' by 23', with the apse coming off one corner.

To the left of the great arch leading into the altar space was another, narrower arch springing from the same level. This would have provided access to a passageway in the thickness of the east wall of the keep which led though ultimately into the great hall. This narrow arch is placed at a peculiar angle, as though the wall plane in which it was set was meant to funnel the attention of a spectator standing in the northern part of the nave towards the altar. But if this is the correct reading of the thinking behind the arrangement along the east end of the chapel, it still has to be acknowledged that it is designed to compensate for a problem which could have been avoided altogether by placing the altar where one would expect it, in the centre of the east wall, perhaps in a rectangular recess as happens at Castle Rising. It may be that the desire to have an apsed and vaulted recess of some depth so dominated the patron's or the designer's view of what was appropriate that the eccentric placing of the altar, in a corner and facing south east, was adopted despite the difficulties it brought in its wake. It is worth reminding ourselves that both the great keeps designed in the previous generation, at the Tower of London and Colchester, had apsed and vaulted altar spaces, and that square altar enclosures, like that at Castle Rising Castle in the mid twelfth century, were also very rare in cathedrals, monasteries or parish churches in the thirty or more years after the Norman Conquest. Thus, while the position and character of the altar space have, at least in part, to be seen as surviving from an earlier stage in the planning of the keep, a conscious decision was made to leave that element in its original form rather than adapting it to fit in with the redesigned and enlarged rectangular nave.

The Chapel Anteroom

Adjacent to the chapel on its north side there was, almost certainly, a substantial chamber some 12' by 27'. At Castle Rising, which is so heavily dependent on Norwich in its internal organisation, there is a comparable room in this position. The ceiling of the anteroom was probably at the same height as that of the chapel, but it meant that the room could have had no direct access to an outside wall in which to place a window to light it. Perhaps, as at Rising, there was an opening towards the hall, through which it borrowed light. If there were a priest or priests who required separate accommodation within the keep, this might be a convenient position for them, but there is no direct evidence that this was the case and so the suggestion should be treated with caution. It is equally possible that, with potential access to the well at its west end and the hall to the north, the space was not living accommodation at all but part of the provision of services for the principal dining room.

We have now completed a circuit of the main public spaces in the eastern two thirds of the keep at main floor level. Although there are some uncertainties in reconstructing these rooms, enough can be seen in the surviving fabric or deduced by comparison with other monuments to allow a degree of confidence about the original arrangements. As we move west down the hall beyond the wood partition which screened off the west end of the building we enter areas where both the physical structure and the function of the spaces are less clear. One is to some extent the result of the other: if the intended functions of the rooms were known it might help clarify their forms, and vice versa. Nonetheless, some characteristics can be determined, especially in the kitchen and latrines.

The Kitchen

Before the keep had reached first floor level, a decision was taken to suppress the spiral staircase which had been begun in the north-west corner of the building, to floor it over, and to use the corner which was to have contained it for a large fireplace. How much of what we see today in the area surrounding the fireplace was part of the original design and derived from the imperatives of circulation attendant on the presence of the stair, and how much is a result of adapting the space to a kitchen is not entirely clear. Nonetheless, some elements in the developing process can be quite fully understood. For example, the masonry vaults, remains of which still project from the walls around the fireplace, might be regarded as part of the revised scheme, designed to reduce the risk of fire. However, since all the indications are that the south-west corner, where there was no fireplace, had an almost identical arrangement we may fairly deduce that the complex sequence of groin vaults over the kitchen was envisaged even before the decision to convert the space into a kitchen was taken. It is indeed likely that the peculiar, wedge-shaped vaults across the corners of building in the lower level of the keep were intended to support a stone wall above, part of the purpose of which was to receive the weight and thrust of the vaults to be built at first floor level. The principal changes which must have occurred as a result of deciding to have a kitchen in the keep were thus limited to the provision of smoke outlets in the corner, and the blocking of a passage in the thickness of the north wall originally intended to provide access to the spiral staircase. A further alteration, the purpose of which is less clear, was the provision of a stone screen from the wall to the south of the fireplace. It ran east west, was pierced by at least one arch and stood to a height of about eight feet. It bears no relation to the vault above, or to any other extant feature. Its effect must have been to create two parallel aisles within the kitchen, one with the fire at its west end, the other with a window recess.

Room A

Access to the kitchen was gained from an irregularly shaped room, which was roughly a half octagon with a floor area almost 600 square feet, the function of which is unknown. The traces of beaker moulded blind arches on coursed columnar supports on its west wall suggest that this space was for rather more than the storage of provisions or the preparation of food. In other words it is probably not a pantry or buttery, such as one might expect at the end of a hall in the later medieval period. The possibility that it was open to the roof and well lit by the array of windows in the west and north walls of the building would also distinguish it from the service rooms adjoining later halls, but given that all that actually remains of it is the short stretch of blind arcading already mentioned, we are never likely to know much about it. It always has to be borne in mind, however, that some function must have been envisaged for it in the period before the decision was taken to insert a kitchen, so that if it ever became a service room that too was quite probably an afterthought. A room with an identical floor plan in mirror image existed to the south of the spine wall (room B), but its function must have been rather different from the outset.

The Latrines

Also accessible beyond the main screen wall across the interior were the latrines, of which there were four compartments, each containing four units. It seems that only two compartments could be reached directly from the northern half-octagonal room (room A) just discussed. They were placed in the thickness of the wall as too was the corridor which gave access to them, and the corridor itself was provided with an entrance vestibule, lit by a window. The quadripartite groin vaulting which covered the vestibule and the two compartments and divided the corridor into bays suggests a desire for architectural embellishment of this important convenience. The vaulting of the corridor is particularly significant, for the wall passages in the building are generally barrel vaulted. It is only when they are meant to indicate the possibility of a change of direction that a cross vault is put in. Thus for example, when a window recess crosses a wall passage it is topped by a quadripartite vault to show the two directions of view. The placing of such vaults over the corridor to the latrines thus draws attention to the fact that there is an opening off to the side which leads into the latrine compartment. It may seem a minor detail, but it is one which speaks volumes about the care lavished on the design and execution of the building and the thought given to conveying quite subtle visual messages by the deployment of architectural forms.

The Spine Wall Chamber

Between the two pairs of latrine compartments in the west wall of the keep is a window recess which seems originally to have led off and lit a smaller half octagonal room at the west end of the spine wall. Access to it must have been from one or both of the larger half octagons to either side of it, though unlike them, it seems it had its own ceiling rather than being open to the main roof. At Castle Rising the comparable space is accessible only from the room to the south, and if the same was true at Norwich then it is quite likely that the two larger irregular rooms (A and B) did not communicate directly, that to the south being accessible only from the great chamber just as that to the north was from the hall.

Room B and the Lobby

The irregular half-octagonal room south of the spine wall was an important space for controlling circulation around the keep. In its south wall can still be seen a doorway decorated with beaker moulding on its arch and flanked by columns. This door led to the wall passage which in turn lead to the spiral staircase in the south-west corner of the building and thence up to the gallery passage, the roofs and battlements, and down to the basement. The decoration of the door and the provision of five windows in the short stretch of corridor beyond it are indicative of a status rather greater than that given to the stair door in the north-east corner, leading off the great hall.

Also leading from room B was an elaborately vaulted lobby which gave access to an exterior door at the south end of the west wall. Unlike the main door to the great hall, the lobby door is embellished on its interior in the expectation that people would approach from the inside on their way out rather than primarily from the outside on their way in. The wall separating the lobby from room B must have contained the door which gave access to the lobby and it is reasonable to suppose that this was also decorated in some way. The same wall perhaps also contained a window to borrow light from room B to illuminate the lobby. Since the lobby was vaulted above and its only exterior wall was occupied by a doorway (no doubt usually kept shut), it would have lacked any source of natural light unless that derived from the adjacent room. The archaeology of this area of the building is still in need of some clarification so that the interpretation just given may need revision, but the interpretation offered here seems the least problematic of those so far proposed.

The access to the other pair of latrine compartments must also have been from room B, somewhere on its west wall, and if the spine wall chamber also had an entrance within it then there were five doors leading from it. We may therefore consider it as the hub of the southern half of the building, and as that can reasonably be regarded as the more secluded and private part, away from the hall and kitchen, room B must have been the major circulation space for the regular inhabitants. Like the similarly shaped room to the north of the spine wall (room A) it was well lit by windows in two exterior walls, and also like room A, it had substantial mezzanines above it which could be reached by way of the spiral staircase.

The Gallery Passage and Mezzanines
A passage in the thickness of the wall runs round almost the entire building at heights varying between about 10' and 16' above main floor level. This is referred to here as the gallery passage and it served two main functions: to give access to a number of mezzanine platforms and to allow for the easy opening and closing of the window shutters. As there were ten large double light and twelve substantial single light windows which probably had shutters, a single passageway was by far the easiest means of reaching them.

The mezzanine platforms themselves must have been multipurpose. There can be little doubt that the substantial floor area above the chapel, and also probably above the antechapel room, was a major living space.

The available floor was about 37' by 29' though it is possible that it was divided by a partition wall running east/west on the line of the north wall of the chapel. Along the west wall a series of triangular platforms at mezzanine level served not only to provide potential accommodation but also as the way across the corners of the building from the gallery in the west wall to those in the north and south. This was a necessary expedient since the presence of the spiral staircase in the south-west and the kitchen chimney in the north-west corner meant that the gallery had to be diverted out of the wall thickness and onto the platforms formed by the stone vaulted lobby and kitchen respectively. It seems that this solution to circulation at gallery level had been envisaged from the early stages of the designing and building process. It is otherwise hard to imagine why the corners of the keep had been vaulted at basement level: support of stone walls on the diagonal, themselves supporting masonry vaults across the corners of the keep, being the justification from the outset. But even if necessity was the mother of invention, the designer turned it further to his advantage by providing platforms which, at some 12' deep, were far deeper than necessary for circulation. He also provided similar though shallower platforms abutting the spine wall, where they were not needed for circulation at all, and decorated the faces of the chimney and staircase walls with blind arches. This set of responses is absolutely typical of the taste and intelligence of the architect, whoever he was. Expedient solutions were exploited and played for all they were worth.

The Basement

The spiral staircases in the north-east and south-west corners which lead up to the gallery passage, and thence on up to the roofs and battlements, are also the original means of access to the basement. As far as we can tell, there was no outside entrance at ground level, and this arrangement is certainly what we would expect given the design of other keeps of the period. Doubtless the decision not to have a door directly into the basement was taken for reason of security since from most other points of view it was very inconvenient indeed. The principal function of the ground floor was storage - of food, drink, fuel, and perhaps some additional defensive material such as palisading and shuttering, and military hardware. Barrels of wine or salted meat are very heavy and unwieldy and so too are substantial timbers, and yet they apparently preferred to carry them up the main stairs and down a spiral staircase rather than risk a breach in the exterior wall.

The lowly status of the basement is indicated on the outside by its cheaper and rougher fabric (flint rubble walls) and its provision with narrow windows, little more than slits, and those few in number. These were raised well above ground level, again presumably for security reasons, and can only have shed just about enough light for those working in the basement to see what they were doing. It follows from its function and its limited lighting that nothing in the design of the basement interior is likely to have been done for architectural effect, so that the quite complex arrangements of vaults and walls, with which we will be primarily concerned, was almost certainly determined by the structural requirements of the building. Most obviously this applies to the spine wall, which divided the basement into two equal parts each fractionally less than 77' by 33'. The primary function of the spine was to support the timbers of the roof. Since it was not possible to span the interior (some 78' from north to south) in one, a substantial and solid central wall was needed to make it possible to create two independent roofs in parallel. At main floor level, the spine was exploited, as we have seen, as the division between the hall to the north and the chamber and chapel complex to the south. It also served to support the floor joists.

The most unexpected feature of the basement was undoubtedly the barrel vaults spanning the corners of the building at 45°, and these too had a function which only became obvious at higher levels. In the north-west and south-west corners these vaults provided the masonry platforms for the kitchen and the lobby respectively. Since those spaces were, in their turn, vaulted they needed stone walls to receive the weight, and the upper walls were founded in part on the basement vaults. At a higher level again, the gallery wall passage had to cut across these two corners of the building to avoid the kitchen chimney and a spiral staircase. To do so it made use of the vaults above the kitchen and the lobby. This sequence is typical of the inventive forward planning of the designer. He found a unique solution to an anticipated problem and made the necessary provisions at the outset.

However, the vaulted corners were not confined to the extremities of the west wall. They also occurred on the inner angles of the west wall with the spine wall, and were originally planned in the south-east and north-east corners of the keep (fig. 19). The implications of these vaults in the original scheme and their subsequent handling as the design was rethought require careful analysis.

The obvious interpretation of the vaults at the west end of the spine wall is that they too were to support masonry walls at 45° on the floor above, and that this requirement was again to support a stone vault. As well as having logic on its side, this argument can be bolstered by the fact that the earliest extant plans of the main floor of the keep, published in the eighteenth century, still show walls in these positions. They enclose the room which I have referred to as the spine wall chamber. While we do not know that this was stone vaulted or that it supported a platform at gallery level, these inferences

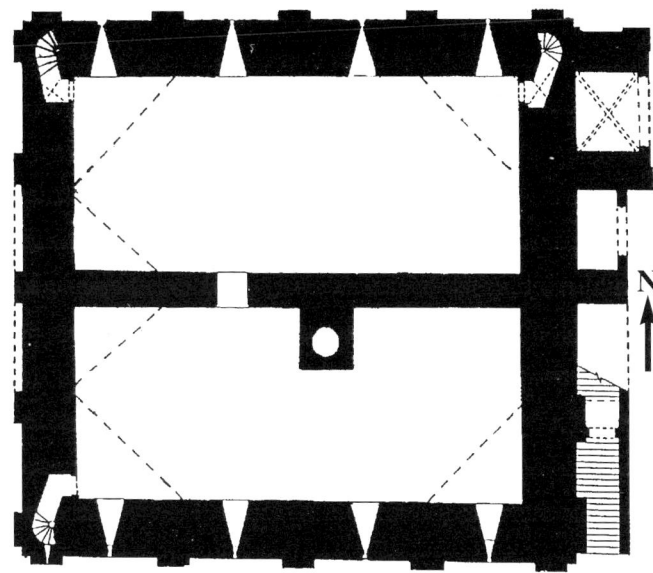

19) Plan of the basement of Norwich keep as originally designed.

are quite reasonable.

Traces of the intention to build a barrel vault in the south-east angle of the keep can clearly be seen on the south wall, however they peter out at about half basement window height. Every piece of original stonework higher up the basement wall indicates that the vault was, in fact, never built. Clearly, then, there was a change of plan in this corner. Logic suggests that the earliest design envisaged that the chapel above would have been limited by the wall which rested on the proposed vault and that it would thus have been triangular in plan, the converging walls of the "nave" leading to the altar space at the apex of the triangle. Such a proposition has the huge advantage of explaining the peculiar placing of the altar space in the chapel as eventually constructed, at an angle off one corner of the nave.

Had the chapel been constructed to its original dimensions it would have been rather small, as well as an odd shape. The decision to enlarge the nave and make it more or less rectangular thus may be seen as convention reasserting itself, and it is tempting to associate the change with the advent of a new monarch, Henry I, who was not as suspicious of things ecclesiastical as his brother William Rufus had been. That is, however, pure speculation. What is clear is that the change of scheme occurred when the easternmost window of the south wall at basement level was about half built. To support the new alignment envisaged for the chapel walls above, two new foundation walls were begun in the basement (fig. 20). One running north south was in the centre of the second bay from the east and would have blocked a basement window in this position. Accordingly another opening was built further to the west through the central buttress of the south wall to preserve the level of lighting originally planned.

The north south wall just mentioned, at some 4' in thickness, would have carried a substantial wall perhaps 3' thick to form the west wall of the chapel above. However, the east west wall in the basement was 10' thick which is far greater than is necessary even to support a vault. Accordingly I have suggested that it

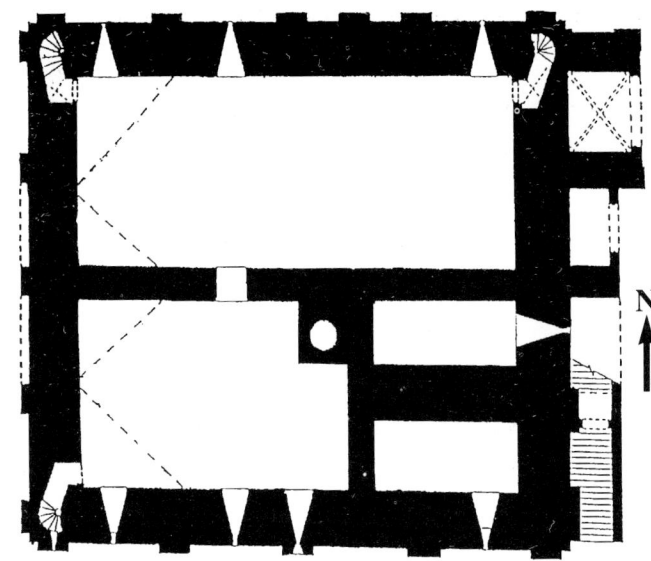

20) Plan of the basement of Norwich keep as first built.

provided the foundation for two parallel walls some 6' apart, the northernmost plain and the southernmost probably with an open arcade to create a north aisle in the chapel above. This cannot be demonstrated other than by the logic that they did not build walls substantially thicker than necessary, and no other obvious solution presents itself.

It was perhaps as part of the same phase of construction that the masonry surrounding the well shaft was inserted. This had the effect of carrying the shaft up to first floor level, which was the height at which it would most often be needed. Whether or not there was also access to the well in the basement is not clear, but the effect of the structure was certainly to block off the entire space in the basement beneath the chapel and antechapel. If these two substantial rooms were to be used at all they would have to have been reached through the floors of the rooms above, presumably by means of stairs of a ladder. Speculation about the envisaged functions of these chambers as prisons, as they were in the later middle ages, is inevitable but unprovable. It is worth pointing out though that before the original scheme (with the barrel vault across the corner) was suppressed there would have been no structural need for these chambers. So if imprisonment was originally planned as a function of the keep alternative provision was presumably made.

The physical evidence for the intention to vault the north-east corner of the basement is less clear than for any of the others. In part this may be because of the early structural failure of the north wall, which led to a substantial campaign of patching and refacing even as the building was going up. However, even though a start was made on providing a vault here, it may well have been abandoned almost immediately since nothing survives more than two feet above the surviving impost level. Symptomatic of the difference between the arrangement here and in the south-east corner is the height of the window arch. That under the chapel is low enough to have accommodated the vault which in the event was never built whereas that in the north-east rises so high that its head would have been obscured if a vault had been placed there. The greatest difficulty in understanding the intention to vault this corner is seeing what possible purpose it could have served, other than to satisfy a desire for symmetry. Anything built upon it at main floor level would have intruded into the space of the hall, so that the most it is likely to have achieved is a strengthening of the floor in the corner between the top of the main stairs and the spiral staircase into the basement, across which the heavy traffic mentioned at the beginning of this section must have travelled. In the circumstances, it is less surprising that it was abandoned than that it was planned to begin with.

In a subsequent phase of construction, perhaps well after the building was completed, both the north and south compartments of the basement were provided with foundations for an arcade running east west along their centres. To judge by scars in the east wall of the north compartment they supported vaults. This may be a subsequent change; in the first instance the arcades may simply have been lending support to the joists of the timber flooring originally installed across the majority of the building.

Conclusions

The interior of Norwich keep reveals some fairly substantial changes of mind which could never be guessed from the outside, probably not even in its prerestored state. Several of the alterations occurred at or a little above the mid height of the basement storey. Most notable amongst them were the change in the plan of the chapel, discussed above, and the suppression of the staircase in the north-west corner so that a large fireplace and chimney could be inserted to provide a kitchen at first floor level. The failure of the north wall must have become obvious at about the same point so that the addition of the sixth buttress on the exterior, with its consequences for the fenestration of the hall above, can also be attributed to this period. What is more striking than the changes of mind, though, are the continuities between the provisions made early on in the building process and the completion of the interior layout. This seems to include such redundant features as the passageway in the thickness of the wall, which would have joined the spiral stair in the north-west corner to room A. The builders pressed ahead with it even after the stairwell had become a kitchen, though they blocked it off to transform it into two separate window niches. Then again, no attempt was made to redesign the southern wall of the chamber to take account of the fact that its symmetry had been compromised by the realignment of the side walls of the room.

One might conclude from such characteristics that the builders went on following an original master plan quite closely in some details despite the fact that the logic had sometimes gone. Indeed, if the thesis to be put forward in the final chapter is correct, and the character of the architecture is to be understood in the context of the tastes and extravagances of William Rufus's court, then it is likely that even the parts of the fabric manufactured well into the reign of Henry I are adhering to a brief defined in the very different climate of the late 1090s. Such a conclusion would not be out of keeping with the continuities of aesthetic found in major churches, construction of which often spanned half a century or more. It is nonetheless an important conclusion, for while the aesthetic unity of a church might be seen as a tribute to God, the perfect architect of the universe, the relentless pursuit of the same ideal in a secular building at first invites a more prosaic explanation. It could indeed have been that the royal administration was not sufficiently in control to have made alterations had it wished to, or even that they were oblivious to what was going on in Norwich. Neither is likely since the constant toing and froing of bishop and earl, Henry's own visits to the city in the first decade of the twelfth century, and the inevitably high cost of the project all point to its being a very conscious decision. Quite probably the budget was prepared and money earmarked from the beginning and there was no need to risk discontent by cutting back on expenditure just because there was a change of regime at national level. Quite probably too the personnel involved in the building provided a continuity which made seeing the original design through to completion the least disruptive option. But there is a final, aesthetic justification which should not be overlooked. The conception of the keep was a harmonious whole. Its lavish decoration and elaborate provision of accommodation and services were designed to work together to create an impression of modernity, luxury and even elitism. To subtract ingredients at random from this heady brew threatened to unbalance the entire recipe. Better by far to go ahead with it, and should anyone voice open criticism it could always be deflected by reminding them that the scheme was part of the previous government's policy.

CHAPTER 4
Romanesque Architecture and Social Context

The Norman Conquest had a dramatic impact on architecture in England. The scale, style and the sheer number of buildings begun in the thirty years after 1066 are inconceivable without the determination of the invaders to place their own stamp of control upon English institutions and landscape. However, that said, the architecture of the Normans in England was always far more than simply that of Normandy shipped across the Channel. For one thing, the buildings constructed in the duchy in the fifty years prior to the invasion of 1066 are sufficiently varied to call into question whether there was a Norman style as such rather than a varying amalgam of responses by Norman patrons and masons to the architecture of northern, central and western France in general as it had been developing over the previous three centuries. "Norman" architecture is thus best understood as a series of experiments within the context of French Romanesque. A second consideration which follows from this is that the effect of importing this experimental approach into England was primarily to broaden the range of stylistic ideas and raw material on which the experiments could be based. Anglo-Saxon architectural attitudes and building techniques were not entirely ignored by the invader, and the Anglo-Saxon tendency to look for ideas in the Low Countries, and further south in Lotharingia was also to affect the Normans.

Ecclesiastical architecture in England has been more carefully analysed for signs of influence than have the varied buildings which we now lump together under the term "castle", but secular architecture was just as inventive and resourceful. A comparison of the earliest parts of Richmond (Yorks), Exeter, Castle Acre and Chepstow castles (to take examples from North, South, East and West) shows a range of responses: to site, to the use of materials, to architectural vocabulary and of course to the political situation, which can scarcely be paralleled in the major churches surviving from the period. To some extent the variations are indeed regional, but features of each of the buildings just mentioned occur in Norwich keep and indeed more widely. Thus the two light window with central column found at Scolland's Hall at Richmond recurs, on a much grander scale, in Norwich and in many other secular buildings. The cushion capitals found in the castle gate at Exeter (probably of 1068) and the blind arcading in the interior of the hall at Chepstow also become widespread and are found in Norwich keep. And the almost square groundplan with spine wall placed almost centrally within it is a feature of Castle Acre, which quite possibly provides the direct source for the plan at Norwich. But, as I hope is already clear from the previous chapters, one cannot understand Norwich, or any major piece of architectural design, as simply a whimsical, "pick-and-mix" composition. The scale and cost of the project, the Castle's importance as an administrative centre and as an image of political dominance were all such that the design could not be left to chance. A series of instructions from the king's court would have informed the architect and his immediate overseer(s) how much was to be spent and what accommodation was expected as a result. It is also likely that indications were given about the decorative character of the building since this was very unusual in a secular context and can hardly have been an independent decision of the builders, not least because of the expense it would have incurred.

There is no doubt that the starting point for the design would have been the massive masonry keeps introduced into England by the Normans, of which the White Tower in London was the prime example. The White Tower itself illustrates many of the characteristics of the Norman approach to architecture. To begin with it is a remarkably ambitious building, for though one can speak of masonry keeps being "introduced" as a result of the Conquest, there was nothing to match its scale or complexity anywhere in France, including Normandy. The idea of a great stone tower as the centrepiece of a lord's residence may well have originated in the Loire valley. Certainly most of the earliest surviving examples, Beaugency, Montrichard, and Montbazon to name but a few, are concentrated in that region.[26] However, they can explain little more than the outline of the idea since they lack both the internal arrangement of several rooms per floor and the articulation with multiple pilaster buttresses defining bays spanned by a single great arch on the exterior. The White Tower is also architecturally eloquent, in that the east end of its chapel is expressed on the exterior by a great apsidal projection which runs the height of the building. By the standards of the 1070s the White Tower is elaborate indeed.

The source of the projecting apse at the Tower is symptomatic of both the opportunism and to some extent the motivation behind the distinctively Anglo-Norman castle keep. It seems that the two earliest great keeps in England, at Colchester and London, were begun at about the same time, in the mid 1070s. Colchester's was founded on the site of a Roman temple to the emperor/god Claudius. Indeed, the foundations of the keep are determined by the outline of the Roman building which included an apsidal projection in its south-east corner.[27] Realising its potential, the Normans used this feature to designate the chapel in the keep at Colchester and were so taken with the idea that they "copied" it at the Tower of London. The motives for building on a Roman site are quite likely to have been to remind the native population that just as England had been subjected by the Romans, who built great, stone buildings, so now it was under the control of the Normans, who built even bigger ones. It is doubtless also significant that the

Claudian temple site had apparently been used for a palace by Anglo-Saxon monarchs, but that had been on a much smaller scale. The notion of Roman imperial triumphalism commandeered by the Normans for their own political purposes is borne out by the site of the White Tower in London, which occupied a corner just inside the Roman city wall and loomed over it. Even the exterior articulation of the Tower with giant order pilasters may be intended to recall great Roman structures such as the imperial basilica at Trier in Germany.[28]

That the great keeps of London and Colchester speak an architectural language of power can hardly be doubted and nor, I think, can the realisation that the language was a response to a very particular situation, that of Conquest. Within Normandy itself such a language was arguably unnecessary, inappropriate, or even offensive, and so it is perhaps not surprising that nothing approaching this scale was contemplated until what amounted to Henry I's reconquest of the duchy. By then the character and probably the perception of the great stone keep had changed significantly, and that change is manifest, in an extreme form, at Norwich.

Even the most cursory comparison of the exteriors will reveal how different Norwich keep is from the White Tower. In place of the simple pilaster arcading of the latter we see the multiplicity of variously moulded arches on coursed columnar supports (described in chapter 2). It is a move from grandeur to intricate sophistication, and one that can be paralleled quite widely in Anglo-Norman architecture, particularly in the greater churches. The English cathedrals whose designs can be dated to the 1090s, most obviously Durham, Norwich and the huge eastern extension at Canterbury, show a similar interest in increasing refinement of detail applied in greater density to the structure. This tendency was not unique to architecture in England, it was a widespread phenomenon throughout western Europe at this period. At the third abbey church at Cluny in Burgundy, begun in 1088, the precise and delicate imitations of Roman Corinthian capitals and fluted pilasters are combined with pointed arches and cusping derived from Islamic Spain (whence also came much of the money to build Cluny). Romanesque architecture was always eclectic, but never more so than in the closing years of the eleventh century.[29]

But not all the symptoms of the interest in increasing complexity and refinement of detail which become prominent in High Romanesque architecture can be found at Cluny. Conspicuous by its absence was the love of convex and concave elements, particularly on arches and their supports, which is such a feature of Anglo-Norman buildings of the period, Norwich keep foremost among them. The enthusiasm for hollows and rolls on mouldings introduces a subtlety in the play of light and shade across the surface of a structure which simply cannot be matched by rectangular section profiles. This is particularly true when, as in England in the 1090s, the rolls are undercut. The distinction between a semicircle and a three-quarter circle on a moulding profile sounds trivial, but for various reasons it is not. A half-column is obviously attached to the surface behind it because no deep shadow is created at the junction to make it stand out. Once there is more than half a circle, the shadows in the increasingly acute angles between projection and wall deepen, and the illusion as well as the reality of depth is greatly enhanced. The arcading on Norwich keep is of this kind, appearing almost to stand free of the wall (hence I use the term quasi-columnar) even though it is in fact built of blocks of stone which course into the sheer masonry of the facades.

The origins, dissemination, and use of quasi-columnar blind arcading in Romanesque architecture have not yet been studied and are thus far from clear. As a decorative device, the blind arcade has been commonplace in European First Romanesque architecture from at least the late tenth century. But in its First Romanesque form the supports are almost invariably flat pilasters, usually in quite low relief. The subsequent adoption of the more visually subtle and expensive columnar forms can probably be attributed to the influence of Mediterranean architecture, though whether that of Antiquity or of the more recent Islamic or Italo-Byzantine styles is not immediately obvious. What is obvious is the skill and the labour involved in cutting each stone for its place in a shaft so that when they are assembled the illusion of a perfect, straight-sided cylinder is created. On the south facade of Norwich keep there were a hundred columns requiring an average of about twelve stones each. When the other facades and the interior are taken into account we may estimate some 4,000 column sections, each cut with precision for its specific location. If we add to this the even more complex arch mouldings which they supported, then we realise, if we have not realised it before, that this is an architectural language of conspicuous consumption and display — a language quite foreign to the Romanesque of the mid eleventh century and only used in the late eleventh for buildings of the very highest status.

The phenomenon at which we have just been looking requires both a general and a specific explanation. In other words: why such sumptuous ostentation in the late eleventh century, and why on a castle in Norwich?

The answer to the first part of the question has to be sought in the context of economic expansion and growth in luxury production that distinguished the late eleventh century. The answer to the second part of the question is also related to this phenomenon. Cities were the principal centres of both consumption and production and as Norwich was the largest town in the most densely populated county in England it was well placed to contribute to and benefit from the growth in economic activity. But though that might explain why the royal administration was prepared to put resources into Norwich it does not entirely account for the extent of the expenditure or the ostentatiousness of the castle that was built there. To understand that more fully it is necessary to look at the character of the royal administration and since at this period that was effectively the king's household, it is likely that in many ways it reflects the predilections of the king himself.

King William Rufus does not have a high reputation among historians. The chroniclers of his own days were nearly all churchmen, and as the king generally had poor relations with the Church (from the papacy and the archbishop of Canterbury downwards) they penned criticisms of him which have coloured the work of almost all subsequent writers. In particular they reproved his court for its licence and its love of luxury, and Rufus received his share of this hostility.[30] One focus of attention was new fashions in male dress which favoured tight-fitting tunics that emphasised thin waists and swaying hips, long skirts split to the waist to reveal the legs right up to the thigh, long cuffs hanging from the wrists, and shoes with long curling toes. A representative anecdote reports that on being presented by his chamberlain with a pair of new shoes which cost three shillings Rufus declared "You son of a whore! Since when has a king got to wear shoes as cheap as that? Go and buy me some for a mark of silver" (thirteen shillings and fourpence).[31] And although the king, who was reputedly thickset and portly, was not well designed for the new fashions, he nonetheless adopted the long hair and centre parting which were part and parcel of this aesthetic of excessive length and revealing splits.

Love of display was not confined to dress and coiffure. The rebuilding of the Palace of Westminster was a major project of the 1090s culminating in the inauguration of the new great hall at Whitsuntide 1099. Although it was remodelled in the late fourteenth century, Westminster Hall as it exists to this day is essentially Rufus's structure. At some 240' by 67'6" it is the largest hall known in Europe at the time, and certainly it remained the biggest in medieval England.[32] However, according to one chronicler, on being congratulated on his achievement Rufus replied that it was not big enough by half! This gives a flavour of his architectural ambitions, and these are borne out by the recovery during the last century of some of the details of the Hall still embedded in the later recasing. It had, for its period, very large window openings at the level of the wall passage above the dado. The openings were framed towards the hall by moulded arches raised on two storeys of columns each with capital and base. Linking these frames were arcades springing from paired columns at the level of the lower capitals, and these formed a continuous sequence of open arches down both sides of the building. Several capitals were discovered during repair work, and these demonstrate a figure style quite similar to that of the doorway to Norwich keep. Both sets contain capitals showing a stag hunt (fig. 14), and possibly also the fable of the wolf and the lamb. The most distinctive motif, however, is the kneeling man with shield and sword or axe which occurs on a capital from Westminster and on a voussoir at Norwich (fig. 12).[33] Such coincidences suggest a common repertoire of visual devices circulating among the masons who worked for the king.

However, despite the comparable interest in architectural elaboration and display, there is no suggestion that Westminster Hall and Norwich Castle keep are the products of the same designer. They share the same rich taste, but not the means of expressing it. Paradoxically, the architecture of Westminster Hall is closer in detail to that of Norwich Cathedral. This is obvious when the two storeys of columns surrounding the clerestory windows of the cathedral are compared with those in the Hall. The similarity may also extend to the arch mouldings, which were generally rather different from those in the keep. So who was the designer, and where did his own particular ideas come from?

The layout of Norwich keep and its overall profile are quite unlike the majority of English essays in the genre. For example it lacks the substantial projections at the corners of its plan which at the White Tower and at most later keeps support towers or at least turrets which project well above the height of the main battlemented walls. By contrast, Norwich employs standard size pilaster buttresses at the corners and probably maintained a single level against the skyline. These two related phenomena are otherwise to be found principally in western France, particularly on the River Loire and its tributaries. Some examples from the eleventh and early twelfth centuries have already been mentioned, Beaugency, Montrichard, Montbazon, and the type continues into the twelfth century at Loches and elsewhere.[34] By that date however the greatest Loire valley castles were becoming very tower-like indeed, and were much taller than they were wide. By contrast, the proportions of the earliest western French examples such as Langeais reveal that they derived from first floor halls. They were essentially two storey structures, a hall above a basement, and thus lacked great height. At first sight, then, it looks as though the designer of Norwich has returned to the origins of keep design in the Loire valley rather than just building upon more recent Anglo-Norman experiments.

Before accepting this view it has to be acknowledged that there are possibly local precedents and that some of the features of Norwich can only be explained by earlier English castles. As has been mentioned, Castle Acre Castle, as first built, had as its principal feature a keep-like structure on an almost square plan and with the spine wall placed almost centrally within it.[35] At first floor level the spine divided the square into a hall and a chamber. Although, so far as we can tell, it lacked an internal chapel, Castle Acre quite probably derives from the White Tower. However, it has no spiral staircases and no buttresses on its corners and is thus unlikely to have had corner towers. Its overall form is thus rather more like Norwich and perhaps therefore a better explanation for Norwich than anything else in England or on the Continent. But Castle Acre is a relentlessly plain, flint and rubble building, and thus provides no sort of parallel for the decorative detailing at Norwich.

As a general phenomenon the blind arcading, intricate moulding and sculpture has already been accounted for. But the desire for increasing elaboration does not explain the form that the elaboration takes. It must be admitted at the outset that some aspects of the forms, for example the beaker clasps, seem to come from nowhere, and they may well be inventions of the designer or his masons. Another remarkable characteristic, which is visible on the main doorway (fig. 11), is the continuation of this arch moulding onto the inner order of columns flanking the opening. This effectively unites the vertical and the semicircular elements of the composition, and is a precocious example of this practice in England. The application of a single decorative device to an arch and its supporting column is common in northern Italy at this period, but there the motifs used are typically a rope moulding, foliate scrollwork or linked circles. There is nothing resembling the beaker clasps at Norwich.

The origin of this motif should probably be associated with the development and use of a kind of arch ornament known as beakhead. The pioneering study of this phenomenon demonstrated that the earliest Romanesque versions of the idea in the form of heads spanning a hollow moulding to link the extrados of an arch with a roll moulding on its inner edge were to be found in western France, for example in the cloister of St Aubin at Angers, just north of the Loire, or on the doorway at Mesland, between Blois and Tours, some eighty miles upstream.[36] These monuments provide us with parallels for other aspects of the Norwich doorway from individual motifs, such as the small "jellymould" bosses, to habits of mind, such as the placing of self-contained and apparently unrelated motifs on adjacent voussoirs (fig. 13), to details of architectural treatment, such as the way in which the roll moulding is placed on the front face of the arch rather than on its corner. But while these parallels probably do substantiate the claim that there was a strong western French connection, the realisation is Anglo-Norman both in overall effect and details of style. For example the insistent repetition of motifs from block to block gives the decoration a quality of hard patterning rarely found outside England and Normandy. And in detail the capitals to the right of the portal show animals entwined in sub-foliate strapwork of Scandinavian derivation which have no parallels in western France; indeed a close parallel can be found in Norwich itself, the cross-shaft fragment from the church of St Vedast.

One way to explain why it is that established local features are found mixed in with designs and ideas from hundreds of miles away is to suppose that native craftsmen were given a relatively free hand in executing details, while the overall conception was that of an architect conversant with recent developments elsewhere in England and France. Such a solution is attractive but runs the risk of underestimating the interplay between local and international in the fundamentals of the design. The possible influence of the castle at Castle Acre has already been discussed, but we should also consider the effect of an even greater building project which was much closer to hand —- Norwich Cathedral. It is at the Cathedral, particularly on the exterior of the north transept facing the bishop's palace, that we find the closest approximation to the serried ranks of arcading which characterise the keep (fig. 21). Although it is true that western French churches, for example, often have their facades covered with blind arches, they generally lack both the lightness (tall, slender columns and small scale mouldings) and the continuity around the building which make the Cathedral's north transept and the keep in Norwich so similar.

We do not know whether it was the former or the latter which first realised the potential of arcading for unifying several facades of a single structure in this way. While it is not without forerunners on church towers,

21) Exterior of the north transept of Norwich Cathedral from the north west.

whether Anglo-Saxon or Norman, it is the two buildings in Norwich that first consciously exploit that potential to the full in other contexts. What we are witnessing is the formation of a distinctive local variant of a style the elements of which can be found piecemeal in England and on the Continent in the late eleventh century. For just as the buildings are unmistakeably High Romanesque they are also specifically East Anglian.

The reason that we now recognise in these monuments the characteristics of a local style is because their regional impact was significant; they were very influential on the buildings that followed them. The great churches of Ely and Bury St Edmunds, both begun before Norwich Cathedral, were altered in design to take account of some of its innovations, and many of the local priory churches (Wymondham, Binham, Castle Acre) are very much dependent upon it.[37] The Castle's principal impact was on the only other square keep built in the county during the Romanesque period, at Castle Rising. In most respects Rising is, as we have seen, a smaller version of Norwich keep. Although it lacks the quantity of decoration or the complexity of internal spacial arrangements of Norwich Castle, it is still much more like it in both respects than any other keep in the country.

Many of the sculptural motifs of the Castle also find their way into the regional repertoire. Versions of the beaker clasps, for example, are found widely on church doorways (Norwich St Julians, Thwaite St Mary, Framingham Earl) and even on towers (Gillingham). At Aldeby, founded as a cell of the Cathedral in 1119 by Bishop Herbert Losinga, both clasps (here rendered as semicircles) and capitals with large upright leaves, like those on the arch into the Castle chapel, are found on the west doorway. There was a free exchange of elements from building to building, as well as the introduction or invention of new motifs. It is perhaps to be expected that the two major buildings in Norwich should set the fashion for the surrounding area, but it is worth stressing that this is what happened because it can be seen that there was no sense in which the patrons of churches avoided using ideas from the Castle. In other words there is little evidence that there were some ornaments perceived as appropriate only for churches or for secular buildings. This reinforces the conclusion that the principal requirement was that Norwich keep be as lavish and as elaborate as was conceivable within the context of Anglo-Norman architecture around 1100 rather than speaking a language that was distinctively secular. However, since such lavishness was nearly always found in an ecclesiastical setting, its use in a military and administrative building must have seemed like an act of appropriation.

Perhaps that is precisely the light in which it should be viewed. The chroniclers of the period refer repeatedly to the diversion of ecclesiastical revenues and resources into the royal coffers. When churchmen pleaded poverty in the face of a substantial tax levied by the king, his courtiers replied "have you not shrines adorned with gold and silver, full of dead mens' bones?", and the king himself is reported to have "feared God but little, men not at all".[38] All Rufus's own inclinations led him to divert money towards secular government and his own image. Thus while the kings of England for fifty years before and after him were known for building monasteries, Rufus was known for Westminster Hall: "he began and completed one very noble edifice, the palace in London; sparing no expense to manifest the greatness of his liberality". But as William of Malmesbury also commented "his liberality became prodigality, his magnanimity pride".[39] Such was the view of a monastic historian who felt that royal largesse should be directed to men of religion, but the king obviously disagreed. "Military men came to him out of every province on this side of the mountains (i.e. the Alps), whom he rewarded profusely".[40] William Rufus took seriously the idea that money was caesar's and should be rendered unto to caesar, and with money came the things that money, increasingly, could buy.

The existence of a workforce trained in the skill of accurate stonecutting, of an administration capable of assembling and co-ordinating the craftsmen and providing materials from (in some cases) hundreds of miles away, and of a designer able to conceive a design as novel and as complex as Norwich keep were recent developments in the late eleventh century. Elsewhere in Europe the consequences of economic and technical developments of this kind are now visible principally in the architecture of churches, but because of the unique equation which brought together a proud secular patron and the expansion of a major city, "celebrated for its trade and populousness",[41] Norwich boasted not only a great cathedral but a castle keep of comparable pretension.

The image which the keep presents is almost totally at odds with modern notions of the dark and forbidding castles of popular imagination. Apart from the self-indulgence of a prodigal king and his fashion-conscious and luxury loving courtiers, was there any rationale behind the expenditure? One justification which can be supported by more or less contemporary evidence is that display on this scale was intended to overawe those who saw it or who lived within its shadow. In the mid twelfth-century <u>Roman de Troie</u>, the poet, Benoit of Ste-Maure describes his vision of the ancient citadel of Troy, built by King Priam:

> It was situated on the highest spot in Troy:
> He who made it was a great master.
> ...
> There was situated Ylion
> from which one could survey the whole county
> ...
> All the square stones of the wall

were of marble, white, violet, sapphire,

...

The windows were made
of purified gold and crystal.
There was no capital or pillar
which has not been moulded
with strange decorations and sculpted
and carved with a chisel

...

When Ylion was completed
it was very rich;
it was situated in a proud place.
With its appearance it threatened everyone:
it could threaten because it feared nothing
except what could come from the sky.

    (Tote rien par semblant manace:
    Manacier puet, que rien ne crient,
    Se devers le ciel ne li vient).[42]

The effect of the materials and the workmanship, of the sheer expenditure on Priam's castle was enough to terrify the minds of onlookers. Our own capacity to be overpowered by such effects is greatly diminished. Although vestiges of such display can still be seen in the precision of the Trooping of the Colour or the aerobatics of the Red Arrows, they are too closely associated with entertainment. But for hundreds or even thousands of years, the human imagination has extrapolated from such highly skilled, well drilled and colourful displays the underlying presence of wealth and organisation which cowed and controlled lesser subject populations or would-be aggressors. Such was the intention behind much of the grandest colonial architecture of more recent times. In effect Norman architecture in England was colonial architecture — designed to overwhelm.

It was to prove unfortunate for the subsequent fate of Norwich keep that the increase in technical expertise which helped to bring it into being would also encourage the development of subtle machines for siege warfare which gradually transformed castle architecture into something outwardly plainer and more substantial. But even within the context of its own period Norwich was very exceptional. It was architecturally the most ambitious secular building in western Europe, a tribute alike to the almost godlike vision of kingship of its patron and to the potential which he saw in the new administrative centre of East Anglia, in Norwich.

Notes

1. The Anglo-Saxon Chronicle, trans. G.N. Garmonsway, London and New York 1953, pp. 134-5, from Chronicle versions E and F.

2. Domesday Book: Norfolk, ed. Philippa Brown (general editor John Morris), Chichester 1984, 116b (1,61).

3. The Charters of Norwich Cathedral Priory, ed. Barbara Dodwell, Pipe Roll Society, 78 (new series 40), 1974, no. 1. It is significant that "Apud Norwicense castrum" is almost certainly the original form, since the use of the ablative case implies that there was a "castrum" in Norwich, where the Cathedral was to be built. There are three options for interpreting castrum: that it was the defensive area of the Anglo-Saxon "burh", that it was the site of the early Norman castle, or (and perhaps the most likely) that it was both, since the Normans frequently made use of pre-existing defenses in the siting of their own fortifications. If this last option is the right one then the sequence of events must have been as follows: i) the Normans arrived in Norwich and built a castle at least partially inside the burh, ii) the Cathedral was built in the same area, requiring the Castle to move to a new site, iii) the Castle we see today is on that new site. For later writers who had no knowledge of this sequence, the phrase "apud Norwicense castrum" was anomalous so they changed it to "apud Norwicum castrum", which would be read appositionally meaning "at the fortified place, Norwich". The implications of this suggestion need further research, but they appear to make sense of, for example, the evidence of Domesday Book, that up to 1086 the Castle was in the borough (see previous note).

4. M.W. Thompson, 'Associated Monasteries and Castles: a tentative list', Archaeological Journal, 143, 1986, pp. 305-21.

5. N.J.G. Pounds, The Medieval Castle in England and Wales: a social and political history, Cambridge 1990, pp. 18-19.

6. Cited by H. Harrod, Gleanings among the Castles and Convents of Norfolk, Norwich 1857, p. 138-9, from the Liber cartarum et placitorum.

7. For the visit c. 1104 see Regesta Regum Anglo-Normannorum 1066-1154, ii, eds Charles Johnson and H.A. Cronne, Oxford 1956, nos 659, 661, 786-7; for c. 1109 ibid. nos 875-6 and cf. 877. The Christmas visit of 1121 is variously recorded, for example in The Anglo-Saxon Chronicle, edn cit. p. 250.

8. For the documentation in general see J. Kirkpatrick, Notes concerning Norwich Castle from a manuscript volume... in the possession of William Herring Esq.,, London 1847 (from manuscript notes made c. 1725); W. Rye, Norwich Castle, Holt 1921; R.A. Brown, H.M. Colvin and A.J. Taylor, The History of the King's Works: The Middle Ages, London 1963, esp. vol. 2, pp. 753-54; and Pounds, Medieval Castle, pp. 46-7, 97, 99, 196, 207-12.

9. For St Benet's, Regesta, ii, no. 1306; for Ely, ibid., no. 1656; and for Bury, Regesta, iii, eds H.A. Cronne and R.H.C. Davis, Oxford 1968, no. 757, and see note 11 below.

10. Regesta, iii, no. 272.

11. David C. Douglas, Feudal Documents from Bury St Edmunds, British Academy, Records of the Social and Economic History of England and Wales, 8, London 1932, nos 64, 90, 183 and The Chronicle of Jocelin of Brakelond, ed. and trans. H.E. Butler, London 1962, pp. 66-8.

12. The full original texts up to the early thirteenth century are available in the editions of the Pipe Roll Society, but can also be found in various secondary sources, particularly Rye, Norwich Castle, and Brown, Colvin and Taylor, King's Works, and see also R.A. Brown, 'Royal Castle Building in England', English Historical Review, 70, 1955, pp. 353-98.

13. Cited by Kirkpatrick, Notes concerning Norwich Castle, pp. 24-5, and Samuel Woodward, The History and Antiquities

of Norwich Castle, London and Norwich 1847, p. 7.

14. A brief comment on the masons' marks by A.B. Whittingham appeared in 'A Note on Norwich Castle', Archaeological Journal, 137, 1980, pp.359-60, and for Whittingham's notes Norfolk Record Office, MC 186/211, 649x3. This work is being reviewed by Dominic Marner whose own research will, I hope, shortly be published.

15. For the building trade in England during the (mostly later) middle ages see Douglas Knoop and G.P. Jones, The Medieval Mason, Manchester 1933, and L.F. Salzman, Building in England down to 1540. A documentary history, Oxford 1952. For building stone David Parsons, ed., Stone: quarrying and building in England, AD 43-1525, Chichester 1990, esp. chapters 13, 'Building Stone in Norfolk' by A.P. Harris, and 14, 'Building a Fine City: The provision of flint, mortar and freestone in medieval Norwich' by B.S. Ayres.

16. Wilkins' original watercolours for his engravings are in the Society of Antiquaries, London, Red Portfolio for Norfolk, and Stone's are in a volume in the Castle Museum, Norwich, CMN 1922.3.

17. Eric Fernie, 'Observations on the Norman plan of Ely Cathedral', in Medieval Art and Architecture at Ely Cathedral, British Archaeological Association Conference Transactions, ii, 1979, pp. 1-7 and Eric Fernie, 'Anglo-Saxon lengths: the Northern System, the perch and the foot', Archaeological Journal, 142, 1985, pp. 246-54.

18. Reproduced in M.W. Thompson, The Rise of the Castle, Cambridge 1991, illus. 7.

19. Reproduced in K.J. Conant, Carolingian and Romanesque Architecture, 800-1200, Harmondsworth 1959 and 1966, p. 78, fig. 23.

20. David Wilson, The Bayeux Tapestry, London 1985, pls 12 and 57.

21. Arts Council of Great Britain, English Romanesque Art, 1066-1200, eds George Zarnecki, Janet Holt and Tristram Holland, 1984, cat. 105e.

22. I am particularly grateful to George Zarnecki for his comments and suggestions concerning the sculpture of the doorway.

23. Vitruvius, The Ten Books on Architecture, trans. Morris Hickey Morgan, Harvard 1914/New York 1960, Book I, ch. 2.ii.

24. Ibid., Book IV.

25. See the plans in the Department of the Environment guidebook, R.A. Brown, Castle Rising, Norfolk, London 1978.

26. A. Chatelain, Donjons romans des pays d'ouest, Paris 1973, and idem, L'evolution des châteaux forts dans le France au moyen âge, Strasbourg 1988, esp. pp. 127-47. For fuller bibliographies on individual monuments C-L. Salch, Dictionnaire des châteaux et des fortifications du moyen âge en France, Strasbourg 1979.

27. Paul Drury, 'Aspects of the Origin and Development of Colchester Castle', Archaeological Journal, 139, 1982, pp. 302-419.

28. Illustrated in J. Ward-Perkins, Roman Architecture, Milan 1974 (English edn London 1988), pl. 319.

29. Hans Erich Kubach, Romanesque Architecture, Milan 1972, (English edns 1979, 1988) discusses the emergence of some of the characteristics of High Romanesque architecture, esp. chapter 3.

30. Frank Barlow, William Rufus, London 1983, provides an excellent introduction to the period and to the king and his treatment by historians.

31. Cited by Barlow, William Rufus, p. 100 from William of Malmesbury, De Gestis regum Anglorum, ed. W. Stubbs, Rolls Series 1887-9, ii, 368.

32. See Brown, Colvin and Taylor, King's Works, i, pp. 43-7.

33. English Romanesque Art, (see note 21), cat 105 illustrates and discusses several of the Westminster Hall capitals and provides references to the earlier literature.

34. In addition to the works cited in note 26, see C-L. Salch, J. Burnouf and J-F. Fino, L'Atlas des châteaux forts en France, Strasbourg 1977, and C-L. Salch, Les plus beaux châteaux forts en France, Strasbourg 1987.

35. J.C. Coad and A.D.F. Streeten, 'Excavations at Castle Acre Castle, Norfolk', Archaeological Journal, 139, 1982, pp. 138-301.

36. F. Henry and G. Zarnecki, 'Romanesque arches decorated with human and animal heads', Journal of the British Archaeological Association, 3rd series 20-1, 1957-8, pp. 1-35; reprinted in George Zarnecki, Studies in Romanesque Sculpture, 1979, item VI.

37. Eric Fernie, An Architectural History of Norwich Cathedral, Oxford 1993, pp 145-53, and a forthcoming paper by Malcolm Thurlby in Norwich Cathedral: Church, City and Diocese 1096-1996, eds Eric Fernie and Christopher Harper-Bill, London 1996.

38. Malmesbury, De Gestis regum, edn cit. pp. 371-2 and 367.

39. Ibid., pp. 374 and 367.

40. Ibid., p. 368.

41. Ibid., p. 386: "Ita Herbertus ... sedem episcopalem ... ad insignem mercimoniis et populorum frequentia vicum transtulit, nomine Norwic".

42. Benoit de Ste-Maure, Roman de Troie, ed. L. Constans, Paris 1904, lines 3047-8, 3055-6, 3063-4, 3073-8, 3089-93. I am very grateful to Dr Olga Grlic for drawing this passage to my attention and for translating it.

Further Reading

Brian Ayres, The English Heritage Book of Norwich, London 1994.

Frank Barlow, William Rufus, London 1983.

R.A. Brown, H.M. Colvin and A.J. Taylor, The History of the King's Works: The Middle Ages, London 1963.

Eric Fernie, An Architectural History of Norwich Cathedral, Oxford 1993.

N.J.G. Pounds, The Medieval Castle in England and Wales: a social and political history, Cambridge 1990.

Derek Renn, Norman Castles in Britain, London 1968.

M.W. Thompson, The Rise of the Castle, Cambridge 1991.

Glossary of Architectural Terms

abacus:
The horizontal slab, usually rectangular in plan, that rests immediately on top of a capital. It is frequently moulded, for example with a chamfer, and is sometimes sculpted with foliate or geometric ornament.

angle roll:
A moulding of circular cross section cut at the junction of two faces of a wall or arch.

arcading:
A row of arches, usually supported on columns, piers or pilasters. See also blind arcading.

ashlar:
Stone that has been worked so that its surfaces are relatively flat and smooth, and meet at a distinct angle.

barrel vault:
a vault of semicircular section.

beaker moulding/
beaker clasp:
The name used in this book to describe a projection which spans a hollow moulding on an arch or its support, usually appearing to clasp or anchor a roll moulding (see figs 9,13).

beakhead:
A bird's or beast's head on an arch or its support, usually appearing to clasp a roll moulding.

blind arcading:
A row of arches, usually supported on columns or pilasters applied to a wall which closes off the arcade from behind.

cavetto:
A hollow moulding of roughly semicircular profile.

chamfer:
A bevel, usually flat, cutting back the corner between two surfaces at right angles to each other.

clerestory:
The uppermost level of windows, usually in a church. Those openings which stand above the height of any surrounding aisles or galleries.

corbel table:
A regular series of block-like projections acting as brackets to support a further projection above.

crenel:
The indented parts of a battlemented parapet (compare merlon).

cross vault:
see groin vault.

cushion capital:
A capital which has a cubic upper part and a hemispherical lower part so as to effect the transition between a cylindrical support and a rectangular abacus.

dado:
The lowest part of the wall in any storey of a building, often corresponding to the area below the windowsill.

extrados:
The upper or outer curved surface of an arch.

gallery:
Here used to denote a mezzanine level constituted by wall passages and adjoining platforms.

groin vault:	A vault formed by the intersection of two or more barrel vaults often crossing at roughly a right angle, hence cross vault.	rib vault:	A vault whose underside is supported by or decorated with cut stone voussoirs, usually at the angled junction between two planes.
merlons:	The upward projections in a battlemented parapet (compare crenels).	roll moulding:	A moulding with a section constituting part of a cylinder.
mezzanine:	A minor storey intermediate in level between two principal horizontal divisions in a building.	skeuomorph:	A design which derives its form from or simulates a functional element originally employed in another medium, for example a fibreglass boat which imitates the ridged planking of a clinker built hull.
palisading:	A wall of upright wooden planks or stakes, each, usually sharpened to a point at the top.		
parapet:	A low enclosing wall at the top of (part of) a building, often with a walkway or gutter behind it.	soffit:	The underside of an elevated element in architecture such as an arch or lintel.
pilaster:	A vertical support of rectangular section projecting from a wall.	string course:	A projecting, thin horizontal moulding running across the surface of a building.
quasi-columnar:	An upright support constituted by more than half the diameter of a cylinder. Not quite a free-standing column but more than a half-shaft.	voussoir:	A wedge-shaped stone, one of several constituting an arch.
quirk:	A shallow incision engraved on a moulding in parallel with the other elements of the moulding.		
reticulation:	A pattern of adjacent diamond shapes, here used of squared stones whose edges are set at about 45 degrees to the horizontal.